The Qatar-Nepal Remittance Corridor

Enhancing the Impact and Integrity
of Remittance Flows by Reducing
Inefficiencies in the Migration Process

Isaku Endo
Gabi G. Afram

THE WORLD BANK
Washington, D.C.

ISBN: 978-0-8213-7050-6
eISBN: 978-0-8213-8787-0
DOI: 10.1596/978-0-8213-7050-6

Library of Congress Cataloging-in-Publication Data

The Qatar-Nepal remittance corridor : enhancing the impact and integrity of remittance flows through reducing inefficiencies in the migration process.
    p. cm.
  Includes bibliographical references.
  ISBN 978-0-8213-7050-6 — ISBN 978-0-8213-8787-0
  1. Emigrant remittances—Qatar. 2. Emigrant remittances—Nepal. 3. Qatar—Emigration and immigration—Economic aspects. 4. Nepal—Emigration and immigration—Economic aspects. I. World Bank.
  HG3968.85.Q28 2011
  332'.04246095363—dc22

                                                                              2011016874

Contents

Figures

Tables

Foreword

Remittance inflows play a crucial role in Nepal's economy. Officially recorded remittances already amounted to almost a quarter of the GDP in 2009. The 2008–09 global economic crisis resulted in slower growth of remittance inflows in Nepal, leading directly to lower disposable income. This is a telling reminder of the importance of promoting a supportive environment for remittances.

Nepali migration continues to increase as workers seek greater economic opportunities abroad. In this quest, Qatar is one of the important migration destinations for Nepali migrant workers. The number of Nepali workers in Qatar has grown significantly—from 125,000 in 2004 to 299,000 by end 2008—making Qatar the second largest host country for Nepali migrant workers after Malaysia.

Prepared in partnership with the Qatar Central Bank and the Nepal Rastra Bank, this report publishes for the first time official data on remittance flows from Qatar to Nepal. The report carefully analyzes the remittance markets and related regulatory frameworks in both Nepal and Qatar—including the migration process from Nepal to Qatar.

In particular, the report attempts to quantify the value of commission transfers from Nepal to Qatar (which are illegal). It identifies how the discrepancies between the labor-related legal frameworks between the two countries directly impact these commission transfers. Based on these key findings and detailed analyses, the report lays out a set of actionable policy recommendations for the respective authorities of Nepal and Qatar.

The policy recommendations focus on improving the scale and impact of remittance transfers; improving the legal and regulatory frameworks in order to clarify the ambiguities in the current migration process and procedures, as well as streamline inefficiencies in the migration process; highlighting the need for an efficient payment system infrastructure, and finally, tackling the limited access to financial services by migrant workers and their families. Underpinning all these focused and technical recommendations is the need for both Governments to address the lack of clarity and weak implementations of laws and regulations.

I hope that this report on the Qatar-Nepal Remittance Corridor will contribute to policy interventions by each authority and will facilitate policy dialogue between the authorities of Nepal and Qatar—and ultimately, contribute to setting up a framework that is more conducive to effective and efficient remittance transfers which play a significant role in supporting poverty alleviation in Nepal.

Susan Goldmark
Country Director for Nepal

Acknowledgments

This report was prepared by a World Bank team led by Isaku Endo and Gabi G. Afram under the guidance of Susan G. Goldmark, Jeane Pesme, Simon Bell, and Ivan Rossignol. The report team included Sheikh M. Wameek Noor.

The authors are grateful for continuing support from senior management of Nepal Rastra Bank and Qatar Central Bank (QCB) including Sheikh Abdullah Saud Al-Thani, Governor of Qatar Central Bank, and Mr. Krishna Bahadur Manandhar, Deputy Governor of Nepal Rastra Bank, Sheikh Khalid bin Saud Al-Thani, Director of Financial Stability and Statistics Department (QCB), and Sheikh Ahmed Eid Althani, Head of Qatar Financial Information Unit. The authors thank Marcos Ghattas of the World Bank for his support throughout the project.

The report's peer reviewers are Saleh Al-Sayegh (Qatar Central Bank), Emiko Todoroki, Hisanobu Shishido, and Dilip Ratha (all World Bank). Aurora Ferrari, Shamsuddin Ahmad, Sabin Raj Shrestha, Harish Natarajan, Luchia Christova, and Ceren Ozer (all World Bank) also provided inputs and comments. Najah Dannaoui provided support in reading and translating laws and regulations in Arabic. The authors also appreciate comments provided by participants at a workshop in Kathmandu in January 2010.

The authors would like to express their gratitude to Sheldon Lippman for his editorial support and to Jeffrey Lecksell and Bruno Bonansea for their support in developing a map. The authors thank Suran Shrestha for administrative and logistical support in the Kathmandu office.

Raul Hernandez-Coss, Isaku Endo, Sabin Raj Shrestha, and Gabi G. Afram were team members of the Qatar-Nepal remittance corridor report which was compiled as a background paper for the Access to Finance in Nepal report.

The report benefited from many interviews in Qatar and Nepal. We thank the following people for their helpful suggestions, comments and valuable information: Ram Prasad Adhikary, Ranjan Agarwal, Rashid Ali A. Al Abdulla, Abdulla Salim Al Ali, Khalid Khalifa Al-Kaabi, Mohammed Saeed Al-Nuaimi, Nabil Abdul Badie A. Alsayed, Moftah Jassim Al-Moftah, Khalid Al-Thani, Anil Baby, Ratna Raj Bajracharya, Arjun Prasad Banjara, Tunga S. Bastola, Rishikesh Bhatta, D. P. Bhattachan, Pradeep Bhattarai, Nirvana Chaudhary, Parshuram K. Chhetri, Chandra Prasad Dhakal, Sthaneswar Devkota, Alaa Eldin M. A. El-Ghazaly, Aruna Fernando, Bhaskar Mani Gnawali, Sunil K. Goshali, Ganesh Gurung, Mahendra Man Gurung, Radha D. Gurung, Syed Baseer Haider, Prakash Mohan Joshi, Sashin Joshi, Munal J. Karki, Rajesh Khanal, Manish Koirala, J. Craig McAllister, Surya Nath Mishra, Mohamed Moabi, Hari Kumar Nepal, Arjun Raj Pant, Ashok Palikhe, Hari Krishna Paudel, Narayan Prasad Paudel, Samseer Poil, Pradyuman Pokharel, Achyut Bhakta Poudel, Ananta Rajbhandary, Ashoke Sjb Rana, Ananta Rajbhandary, Tilak Ranabhat, Mohan Krishna Sapkota, Dharma Raj Sapkota, Anil Shah, Ashish Sharma, Rajendra Prasad Sharma, Rajendra Sherchan, R. S. D. Shekhar, Ajad Shrestha, Ajay Shrestha, Bal Gopal Shrestha, Binod N. Shrestha, Jeewan Babu Shrestha, Rameswor M. Shrestha, Michael Siddhi, Sudanshu Srivastava, Dibakar Thapa, Niraj Thapa, Prakash Jung Thapa, Roy Thomas, Shailendra Upadhyay, and Shikhar Vaidya.

Abbreviations

AML	Anti-Money Laundering
APG	Asia/Pacific Group on Money Laundering
BRCA	Bilateral Remittance Corridor Analysis
CDD	Customer Due Diligence
CFT	Combating the Financing of Terrorism
CTR	Currency Transaction Report
DoFE	Department of Foreign Employment (Nepal)
FATF	Financial Action Task Force
FBIR	Finance, Business, Insurance, and Real Estate
FFT	Formal Fund Transfer
FIU	Financial Intelligence (Information) Unit
FY	Fiscal Year
GCC	Gulf Cooperation Council
GDP	Gross Domestic Product
IFT	Informal Fund Transfer
IME	International Money Express
IMF	International Monetary Fund
KYC	Know-Your-Customer
MENAFATF	Middle East and North Africa Financial Action Task Force
MTO	Money Transfer Operator
NAMLC	National Anti-Money Laundering Committee
NIA	Negotiable Instruments Act
NIDS	Nepal Institute for Development Studies
NLSS	National Living Standard Survey
NPR	Nepal Rupee
NRB	Nepal Rastra Bank
Q-Post	Qatar Postal Corporation
QAR	Qatari Riyal
QCB	Qatar Central Bank
QPS	Qatar's Payment System
RSP	Remittance Service Provider
RTGS	Real-Time Gross Settlement
SMS	Short Message Services
STR	Suspicious Transaction Report
TDS	Tax Deductions at the Payment Source
UAE	The United Arab Emirates
US$	U.S. Dollar

Exchange Rates Conversion

3.64 Qatar Riyal (QAR) / 1 US$	73.04 Nepal Rupee (NPR) / 1US$

Average between February 25, 2008 and February 25, 2009

Executive Summary

This report analyzes the migration and remittance transfer processes in the Qatar-Nepal Corridor in order to provide policy recommendations that would help improve the scale and impact of remittance transfers from Qatar to Nepal, and enhance the efficiency and integrity of migration and remittances in the corridor. The report identifies challenges in the migration process from Nepal to Qatar (related to high migration costs and their financing) and constraints in the remittance transfer process from Qatar to Nepal, which together limit the development and poverty reduction impact of remittance flows to Nepali households.

As this report highlights, the Qatar-Nepal remittance corridor has several distinctive features. First, the majority of remittance flows from Qatar to Nepal are being transferred through officially regulated remittance channels. One of the reasons for this is actually the second feature of this corridor, namely, the officially managed migration process from Nepal to Qatar (as a result of which the majority of migrants are documented workers). The third feature is the contrast between the high competition and low prices of remittance services in this corridor on the one hand, and the contradictory rules and high costs incurred during the migration process on the other hand. Finally, as a by-product of the complex migration process which involves multiple players, financial transfers through informal mechanisms take place from Nepal to Qatar in order to pay the commissions of manpower agencies and middlemen. *Therefore, the main issues in this one are not primarily related to remittance costs or integrity of the transfers, as much as they relate to the implications of the complex and expensive migration process on the development impact of remittance flows.*

Migration from Nepal to Qatar

A decision by the Qatari government to increase the number of Nepali migrants in Qatar opened the door for Nepali migration, which was supported by continued economic growth in Qatar. This decision was made in an attempt to increase the share of Nepali migrants in Qatar, as compared to migrants from other Asian countries. Qatar—with its large gas reserves, double-digit growth rates, big construction projects, and high demand for labor—has become one of the top destinations for Nepali migrant workers.

Along with the pull factors stemming from the growth of Qatar's economy, notable push factors driving migration from Nepal include: continued poverty, high levels of unemployment, political instability, and sluggish economic growth. The combination of push and pull factors has resulted in Nepalis becoming the second largest migrant group in Qatar (with approximately 299,000 Nepali migrant workers at the end of 2008). Many of these workers are employed in the construction and manufacturing industries as unskilled laborers. Their salaries vary according to their skills and the industry where they work, but on average they seem to receive lower salaries than those of other migrants for the same work.

One of the key characteristics of this corridor is that migration from Nepal to Qatar is managed in both countries. Managed and temporary migration has resulted in most Nepali migrants being documented workers, which facilitates their access to formal (regulated) financial institutions. As explained in detail in the report, the migration process from Nepal to Qatar itself involves multiple steps, various fees and commissions, takes time, and includes a number of public and private sector players in both countries.

Challenges in the Migration Process

There are a number of challenges in the migration process from Nepal to Qatar that affect the integrity and impact of remittance flows in the corridor, particularly related to the roles played by manpower agencies in Nepal and recruitment service companies and middlemen in Qatar. Although workers can migrate independently, the majority continue to count on the services of manpower agencies without being prepared with the knowledge and information of the migration process. These challenges are:

First, it seems that contrary to the rules and regulations governing the migration process from Nepal to Qatar, Nepali workers end-up paying high migration fees to recruitment agencies. The problem is caused by discrepancies between regulations, lack of enforcement of these regulations, as well as an unclear mix of legitimate and illegitimate fees. As per the Qatar Labor Law and the Qatar-Nepal Bilateral Agreement on migration, payments by migrants or Nepali middlemen for travel expenses and commissions to Qatari recruitment service companies are illegal. The Qatari employer has to pay these costs. However, Nepali regulations allow Nepali recruitment agencies to collect these fees up to a ceiling of NPR70,000. In reality, the total cost of migration for Nepali workers averages around US$1,216. It takes on average 4–6 months' salary for a Nepali working in the service industry in Qatar to recover this cost. *In order to pay for migration, Nepali workers borrow money from their family members and in 43 percent of the cases from local moneylenders* (who charge high interest rates). As a result, remittances sent by migrant workers during the first year are typically used to repay their migration loans, limiting the amount of remittances available for their families.

Second, this migration process has prompted informal funds flows from Nepal to Qatar, in order to transfer the commissions of middlemen and recruitment agencies. Nepali recruitment agencies use Hundi to transfer these commissions in order to avoid paying the required Tax Deductions at the Payment Source (TDS), and to avoid seeking NRB approval for what is a capital outflow from Nepal. In their turn, Qatari recruitment service companies prefer to receive these commissions through informal methods since these commissions are illegal in Qatar. In addition, there appears to be many unlicensed or unauthorized middlemen providing migrant services in both countries, who prefer to use informal fund transfer (IFT) systems. *The size of these commission flows is estimated to range from US$17 million to US$34 million per annum,* amounting to around 5 percent of recorded worker remittance flows from Qatar to Nepal.

Therefore, while meeting a critical need to place workers with firms, the existence of middlemen and manpower agencies in this corridor has fostered an environment of high fees and illegal activities. Ultimately, the migrant worker bears the brunt of this as higher migration costs. To address these challenges, the following steps can be taken:

1. *Qatari and Nepali authorities should clarify all the steps, procedures, fees and responsibilities involved in the migration process from Nepal to Qatar and should enforce the bilateral agreement.* This will minimize abuse and help ensure that all entities

involved in the process are held accountable. Increased transparency in the migration process will help reduce reliance on middlemen and payment of illegal fees, especially airfare expenses, which would significantly reduce the high migration costs.

2. *Nepali authorities should endeavor to empower migrant workers by equipping them with information on the migration process, fees, and responsibilities, and should provide them with financial education.* In particular, given the large number of Nepali migrants heading to Qatar, as well as the importance of remittance flows from Qatar to Nepal, these financial education programs should be tailored to the Qatari context.

3. *Nepali authorities should encourage the development of commercially-viable and sustainable non-collateral-based migration financing schemes,* whereby banks lend migrants based on a collective repayment guarantee by their manpower agency which is repaid directly by the foreign employer through monthly deductions from the migrants' salaries. Partnerships with MFI could also be piloted to expand the reach of such loans.

Remittance Transfers from Qatar to Nepal

Remittance transfers from Qatar to Nepal have been growing steadily since 2001. In 2009, remittances from Qatar to Nepal surpassed US$634 million (or around 21 percent of Nepal's overall remittance inflows). From 2004 to 2006 these flows even grew by more than 100 percent a year (albeit from a low base). However, the onset of the global financial crisis seems to have decelerated the increase in Nepali migration to Qatar and resulted in slower growth of remittance flows since 2008.

Surprisingly, although Nepali workers constitute more than a quarter of the migrants in Qatar, their share of total recorded remittance flows from Qatar remains quite low at about 7 percent in 2008. This paradox maybe partially explained by the type of jobs and lower pay that Nepali workers receive, or the continued (though small and diminishing) use of informal fund transfer channels.

Remittance Service Providers (RSPs) in Qatar are exchange houses, banks, and the postal service. However, exchange houses play a leading role, particularly in the Qatar-Nepal remittance corridor, where exchange houses account for 99.8 percent of the market share. Recent years have witnessed a surge in the number of remittance market players in Qatar, which has resulted in increasing competition, thereby significantly reducing average prices for remittance services in the corridor. Thus most banks do not view remittances as an attractive product and an entry point for marketing other financial services. Given the fierce competition international money transfer operators (MTOs) have seen a gradual decline in their market share, and Money Gram has left the market altogether.

The remittance market in Nepal is relatively well-developed, with a number of banks, money transfer operators and other institutions providing remittance services. The combined market share of non-bank RSP's and international MTOs is estimated at around 70 percent, while banks account for the bulk of the remaining 30 percent. Despite the large remittance market, only a few Nepali banks have entered this market. Nepal Post (which is also principal agent of Western Union) has a very low market share due to lack of automation and slower services.

Because of the increased competition in both the Nepali and Qatar remittance markets, the fees for sending remittances from Qatar to Nepal have decreased by about 50 percent over since 2001. The current average cost for a remittance transfer in the corridor is 3.41 percent for a US$200 remittance transfer (2.89 percent for the fee + 0.52 percent for FX margin). This compares favorably to the global average price of a US$200 remittance transfer, which was 8.83 percent in the first quarter of 2010.

Challenges for Remittances in the Corridor

Most remittances from Qatar to Nepal are transmitted through formal financial institutions such as exchange houses (MTOs) and banks that are regulated by the central banks. The gradual reduction in remittance transfer costs in this corridor has been accelerated by intense competition and increased volumes. However, the following challenges remain.

First, Qatari banks are generally not interested in entering the remittance market, while there remains limited RSP Infrastructure/Coverage outside Doha. Most Nepali migrant workers still feel compelled to travel to Doha to send remittances. In addition, since the services offered by exchange houses are cash-based services, many Nepali migrant workers do not have the opportunity to access savings accounts, which could provide them with safety and enable them access to other financial services.

Second, distribution of remittances in Nepal is constrained by the underdeveloped domestic payment system infrastructure. Nepal is largely a cash-based economy having no electronic funds transfer network for interbank payments. The manual and paper based processes have added to the cost of processing remittances by agents and their RSPs, which has led RSPs to maintain large agent networks to pay cash to recipients (and to aggregate their payments to these agents to minimize credit transfer charges). Both of these have resulted in agents having to be out-of-pocket for longer periods and therefore charging RSPs higher commissions (which translate to higher remittance costs). To address these challenges, the following steps can be taken:

1. *Nepali authorities should expand and upgrade the domestic payment systems and remittance distribution network in Nepal.* They could do so by encouraging banks to increase banking penetration (especially in rural areas) using new technology such as mobile payment schemes, prepaid cards and agent banking solutions. They should also promote the development of an Automated Transfer System for credit transfers which would enable RSPs to move funds to their agents faster and process credit-to-account remittances efficiently.

2. *Qatar Central Bank should encourage exchange houses to open new branches closer to migrant workers locations.* This would reduce the need for migrant workers to travel to Doha to send remittances, thereby minimizing the risks of carrying cash.

3. *Qatari authorities should encourage Qatari firms to open bank accounts for their workers and deposit their salaries in those accounts.* The use of bank accounts to deposit salaries could reduce Qatari firms' costs of handling cash, and would increase workers' security as well as enhance their access to financial services.

4. *Qatari and Nepali authorities should consider supporting the development of remittance services through mobile phones* by developing an appropriate regulatory framework to support such a development in consultation with the private sector, and based on the best practices from other countries' experiences in this field.

The Regulatory Framework for Protecting the Integrity of Remittances

Qatar Central Bank is the regulator and supervisor of banks and exchange houses which provide remittance services. Exchange houses are required to obtain a license from Qatar Central Bank (QCB) and there are multiple requirements for obtaining the license. The Financial Information Unit is the national center for AML/CFT. Of the RSPs, banks and exchange houses are covered under the relevant AML Laws, while, the postal administration is not.

Nepal Rastra Bank is the regulator and supervisor of banks and MTOs in Nepal. The circular for remittance services covers eligibility requirements, certain operating guidelines, specifies reporting and AML/CFT requirements and guarantee requirements. AML laws and directives cover banks and MTOs (but not Nepal Post) and require RSPs to file currency transaction reports (CTRs) and suspicious transaction reports (STRs). A Financial Information Unit (FIU) was set-up at NRB to process this information.

The legal and regulatory framework for remittance services in both Qatar and Nepal seems conducive to enhancing the integrity of these transfers. However, the continued use of *Hundi* for sending migration commission raises integrity concern. In addition, Nepali banks and money transfer operators appear to have weak compliance capacity and need more training of compliance officers. Over-reporting of STRs is taking place and could reflect weak compliance capacity and lack of proper understanding of STR filing. *Finally, the licensing requirements in Nepal should ensure that only financially sound RSPs enter the market.* The current level of bank guarantees might not be adequate to cover the liquidity risk of large RSPs.

To address these challenges, both the Qatari and Nepali authorities should provide effective training on AML/CFT requirements to banks, money transfer operators and other reporting institution. In addition, given the predominance of cash-pay-outs in Nepal, and in order to mitigate potential liquidity risks, the NRB should consider raising the current level of bank guarantee required by non-bank RSPs.

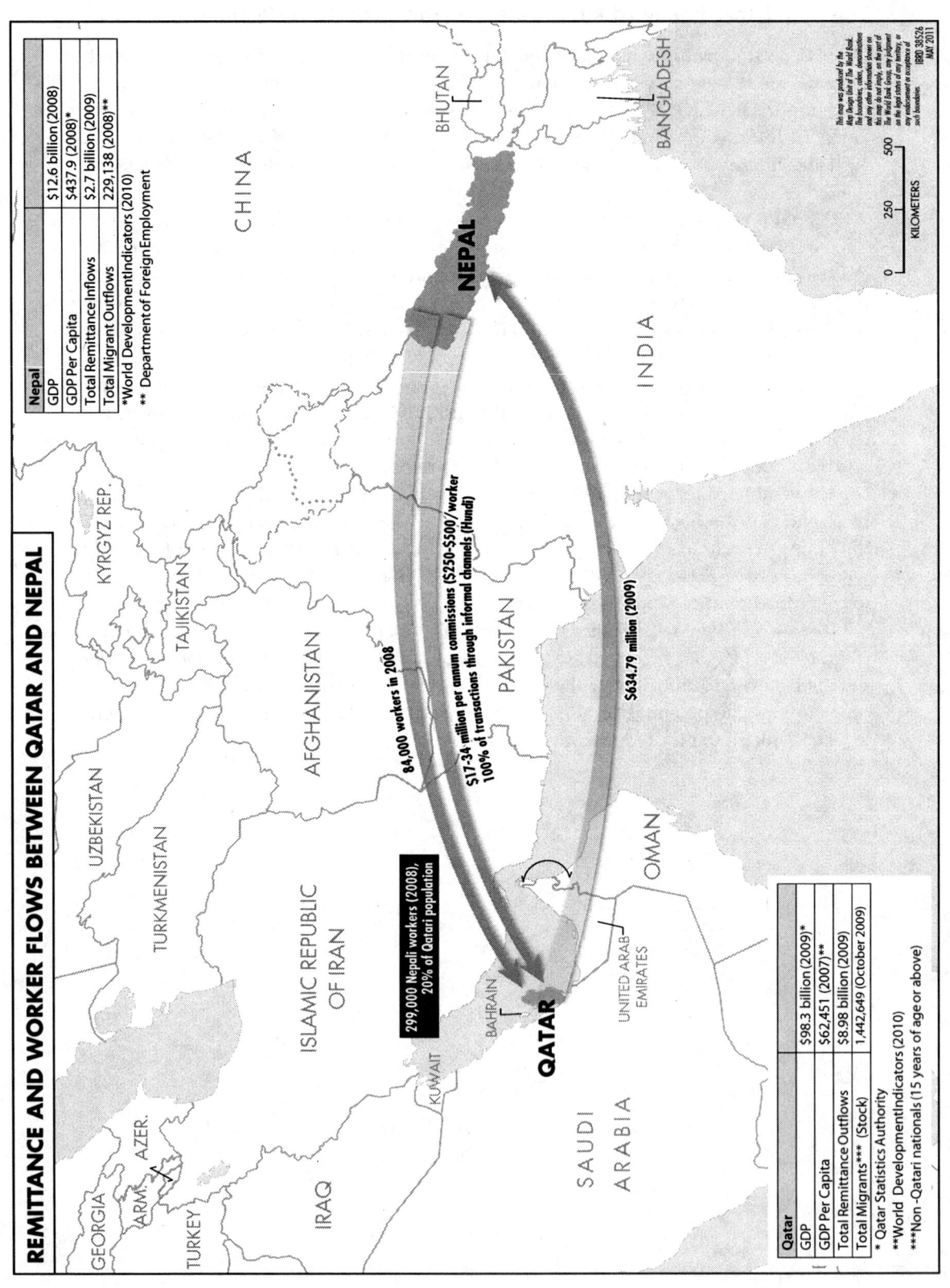

REMITTANCE AND WORKER FLOWS BETWEEN QATAR AND NEPAL

Nepal	
GDP	$12.6 billion (2008)
GDP Per Capita	$437.9 (2008)*
Total Remittance Inflows	$2.7 billion (2009)
Total Migrant Outflows	229,138 (2008)**

*World Development Indicators (2010)
** Department of Foreign Employment

Qatar	
GDP	$98.3 billion (2009)*
GDP Per Capita	$62,451 (2007)**
Total Remittance Outflows	$8.98 billion (2009)
Total Migrants*** (Stock)	1,442,649 (October 2009)

* Qatar Statistics Authority
**World Development Indicators (2010)
***Non -Qatari nationals (15 years of age or above)

84,000 workers in 2008

$17-34 million per annum commissions ($250-$500/worker
100% of transactions through informal channels (Hundi)

$434.79 million (2009)

299,000 Nepali workers (2008),
20% of Qatari population

GEORGIA
TURKEY
ARM. AZER.
IRAQ
ISLAMIC REPUBLIC
OF IRAN
TURKMENISTAN
UZBEKISTAN
KYRGYZ REP.
TAJIKISTAN
AFGHANISTAN
CHINA
NEPAL
BHUTAN
BANGLADESH
INDIA
PAKISTAN
SAUDI
ARABIA
KUWAIT
BAHRAIN
QATAR
UNITED ARAB
EMIRATES
OMAN

This map was produced by the
Map Design Unit of The World Bank.
The boundaries, colors, denominations
and any other information shown on
this map do not imply, on the part of
The World Bank Group, any judgment
on the legal status of any territory, or
any endorsement or acceptance of
such boundaries.

IBRD 38526
MAY 2011

0   250   500
KILOMETERS

Introduction

Background

As migration from Nepal picked up dramatically over the past decade, recorded remittance inflows increased many-fold to reach US$2.7 billion or around 22 percent of GDP in 2009. Qatar—with its huge gas reserves, double-digit growth rates, big construction projects, and large demand for labor—has become one of the top destinations for Nepali migrant workers. *As a result, Nepalis are currently the second largest migrant group in Qatar and send home more than 21 percent of the overall recorded remittance flows to Nepal.* The impact of these flows on Nepal's economy and households has been substantial.

Given the importance of this remittance corridor to Nepal's economy and households, the Nepal Rastra Bank originally requested the World Bank to investigate this corridor in the context of the work on the report on Access to Financial Services in Nepal. As this corridor increasingly became important for both countries, the World Bank decided to update the report by building on initial research and conduct further analysis in order to identify the main issues and provide a set of useful policy recommendations to the relevant authorities to improve the efficiency and impact of remittance flows in this corridor. This study has close links and feeds into the World Bank's flagship report "Large-Scale Migration and Remittances in Nepal: Issues and Challenges." Further, this report draws upon and complements the assessment of Nepal's remittance market based on the *General Principles for International Remittance Services* which was undertaken by the World Bank in 2009.

As this report will highlight, the Qatar-Nepal remittance corridor has several distinctive features. First, the majority of remittance flows from Qatar to Nepal are being transferred through officially regulated remittance channels. One of the reasons for this is actually the second feature of this corridor, namely, the officially managed migration process from Nepal to Qatar (as a result of which the majority of migrants are documented workers). The third feature is the contrast between the high competition and low prices of remittance services in this corridor on the one hand, and the contradictory rules and high costs incurred during the migration process on the other hand. Finally, as a by-product of the complex migration process which involves multiple players, financial transfers through informal mechanisms take place from Nepal to Qatar in order to pay the commissions of manpower agencies and middlemen. Therefore, the main issues in this one are not primarily related to remittance costs or integrity of the transfers,[1] as much as they relate to the implications of the complex and expensive migration process on the development impact of remittance flows.

Objectives

This report identifies challenges in the migration process from Nepal to Qatar (related to high migration costs and their financing) and constraints in the remittance transfer process from Qatar to Nepal, which together limit the development and poverty reduction impact of remittance flows to Nepali households. The report analyzes migration practices, remittance transfer processes, and their underlying legal and regulatory framework in the Qatar-Nepal Corridor in order to provide policy recommendations that would help improve the scale and impact of remittance transfers from Qatar to Nepal, and enhance the integrity of migration and remittances in the corridor. These recommendations are especially important given that although Nepalis constitute around a quarter of the migrant labor force in Qatar, they send home only 7 percent of total remittance outflows from Qatar.

Methodology

This report was prepared through background research (data mining and analysis, literature review, collection and analysis of relevant information/laws), and field work in Nepal and Qatar (where interviews and focus groups were conducted with all stake-holders including: relevant authorities, major institutions, private sector players, returning migrants and their families, and migrant workers). In addition, the following surveys were undertaken: a) a field survey of Nepali migrants in Qatar,[2] b) a survey of both NRB and QCB on regulating and supervising of remittance service providers,[3] c) a survey of NRB on remittances,[4] and d) a survey of selected remittance service providers in Nepal.[5]

Outline of the Report

The report is organized into four chapters. In Chapter 1, the process of migration from Nepal to Qatar is explained and analyzed. Chapter 2 looks at the remittance transfer process from Qatar to Nepal. Chapter 3 provides an overview of the legal anwd regula-tory framework underpinning remittance transfers in both in Nepal and Qatar. Finally, Chapter 4 summarizes the main findings, identifies the main challenges and provides policy recommendations on how to improve the efficiency of the migration and the scale and impact remittance transfers in the corridor.

Notes

1. The integrity of remittance flows means that remittance flows are protected from illicit flows and abuse of remittance channels for illicit purposes.
2. Undertaken by authors in Qatar in 2005.
3. Undertaken by the World Bank (BRCA Horizontal Review Study Group—FPDFI) in April 2010.
4. Undertaken by the World Bank (South Asia Financial and Private Sector Development) in 2009.
5. Ibid.

CHAPTER 1

The Migration Process

This chapter analyzes the migration process from Nepal to Qatar and attempts to answer the following questions:

- *What are the migration trends specific to the Qatar-Nepal remittance corridor?*
- *Who is involved in the migration process? What roles do they play?*
- *What are some of the challenges associated with the migration process from Nepal to Qatar, and what initiatives have been implemented to help overcome those challenges?*

Migrant Workers in the Gulf Region

The Gulf Cooperation Council (GCC) countries are the third-largest destination region in the world after North America and Europe for migrants. Over the past forty years, the six GCC member states[1] have seen the size of their migrant population increase sharply from 1 million migrants in 1970 to 12.8 million in 2005—half of whom lived in Saudi Arabia. In 2010, the total number of non-national migrants in the six GCC countries is expected to surpass 15 million,[2] as illustrated in Table 1.1 below.

This consistent increase in the number of migrant workers to GCC countries as a result of strong economic growth has translated into an estimated US$42.9 billion in remittance outflows from the GCC countries in 2008.[3] This accounts for about 13 percent of global recorded remittance outflows to developing countries, estimated at US$335 billion in 2008 (World Bank, 2010). In the Gulf region, Saudi Arabia is the largest originating country, accounting for US$16.1 billion or 37 percent of GCC remittance outflows in 2008.

Qatar has the largest percentage of non-nationals as a percentage of its total population in the world (Figure 1.1). In 2009, non-Qatari nationals accounted for 89.9 percent

Table 1.1. Size of the non-national population in GCC countries, 1970–2010 (thousands)

Country	1970	1980	1990	2000	2005	2010*
Bahrain	38	103	173	254	295	315
Kuwait	468	964	1,560	1,388	1669	2098
Oman	40	10	450	606	628	826
Qatar	**63**	**157**	**345**	**461**	**637**	**1305**
Saudi Arabia	303	1,804	4,220	5,136	6361	7289
U.A.E	62	737	1,556	2,286	3212	3293
Total	**974**	**3,946**	**8,305**	**10,131**	**12,802**	**15127**

*Estimates.
Source: United Nations, Department of Economic and Social Affairs, Population Division (2009).

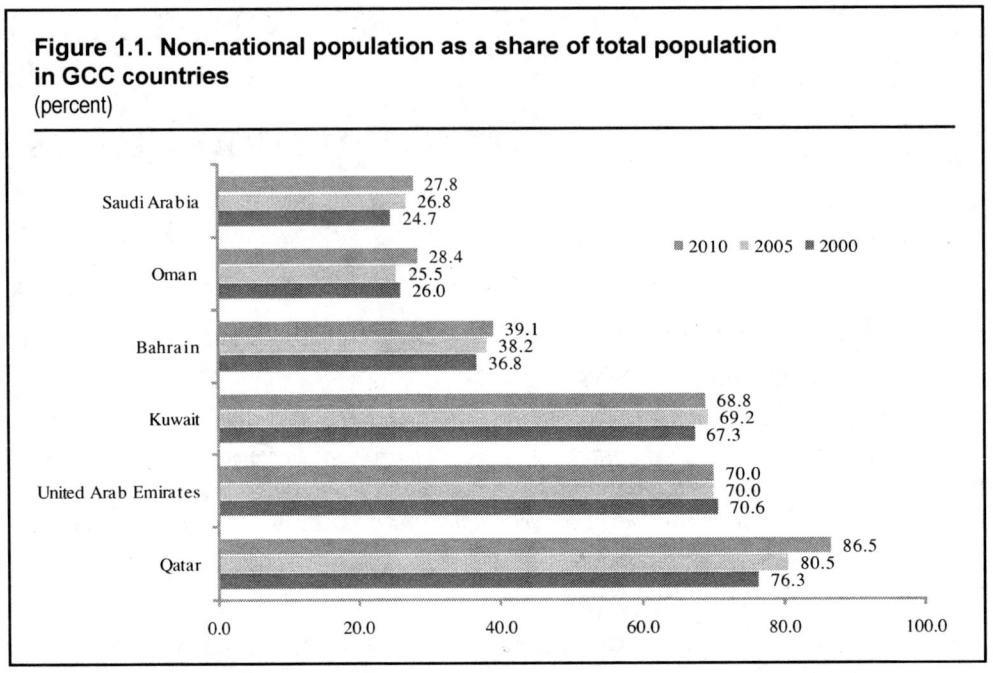

Figure 1.1. Non-national population as a share of total population in GCC countries
(percent)

Source: United Nations (2009).

of the population of 15 years of age and above (see Table 1.2 ; Qatar Statistics Authority, 2010).

Migration of Nepali Workers to Qatar

A decision by the Qatari government to increase the number of Nepali migrants in Qatar opened the door for Nepali migration, which was supported by continued economic growth in Qatar. This decision was made in an attempt to increase the share of Nepali migrants in Qatar, compared to migrants from other Asian countries. Meanwhile, Qatar's economy has continued to grow rapidly over the past five years. According to the IMF, Qatar's real GDP growth was 9.2 percent in 2009, compared with 15.8 percent in 2008 and 13.7 percent in 2007. The IMF also projects a real GDP growth rate of 18.5 percent in 2010. The construction sector has been a key driver of this boom—growing by 24.1 percent in 2008 after a 22 percent growth in 2007. This sector has the highest demand for labor, as it mainly attracts unskilled migrant workers, and is set to continue growing.[4] Along with economic pull factors on Qatar's side, notable push factors driving migration from

Table 1.2. Trend in breakdown of nationals vs. non-nationals in Qatar's population

| | Population (over 15 years of age) | | | | Economically Active Population | | | |
	2004		October 2009		2004		October 2009	
Qataris	110,405	19.2%	146,304	10.1%	52,895	11.9%	72,288	5.7%
Non-Qataris	466,006	80.8%	1,296,345	89.9%	391,238	88.1%	1,193,144	94.3%
Total	576,411	100%	1,442,649	100%	444,133	100%	1,265,432	100%

Source: Qatar Statistics Authority (2010).

Nepal include significant poverty, high-level of unemployment, political instability and sluggish economic growth.

Main Characteristics of Nepali Migrant Workers in Qatar

At the end of 2008, there were around 299,000 recorded Nepali workers in Qatar.[5] Nepalis constituted the second largest migrant group in the country after Indians. The number of Nepali workers has more than doubled since 2004 when there were 125,000 workers. Interviews with the Nepali community suggest that there may be about 15,000 undocumented Nepali workers because of overstay.

Many Nepali workers are employed in the construction and manufacturing industries as unskilled laborers. Others work in the service industry as security guards, hotel staff, taxi drivers and restaurant workers. Nepali workers are mostly concentrated in Doha and the Industrial Area surrounding it. However, they are also employed across the country including at the North Gas Field.

Nepali migrants' wages vary according to their skills and the industry where they work. Unskilled workers receive an average of US$137–220[6] per month, while skilled workers earn an average of US$275–687 per month.[7] Some companies in Qatar provide complimentary accommodation and food for their employees. The table below illustrates random examples of salaries in certain industries in Qatar.

It seems that Nepali migrants in Qatar receive lower salaries than other nationals for the same work. This is due to a number of reasons. First, although the Embassy of Nepal in Qatar (which attests migrant-workers' contracts) has set minimum wages for Nepali workers (as per the requirements of Nepal's Foreign Employment Act-FEA), it is not easy to enforce this. Second, the visa quota limiting the number of Nepali nationals in Qatar has resulted in growing competition among manpower agencies in Nepal, which translates into lower salaries too. Finally, in rural and remote areas of Nepal, a limited number of manpower agencies exist. Thus, Nepali migrants from these areas do not have many choices and whatever conditions and destinations offered are accepted, especially since they do not have information on migration process and fair compensation in destination countries.

Table 1.3. Examples of monthly salaries of Nepali workers in Qatar

Industry	Monthly Salary (US$)	Industry	Monthly Salary (US$)
Trading	689	Restaurant	412
Food	549	Hotel	330
Hotel	275	Trading	247
Petrol Mining	179	Municipality	220
Service	165		
Construction	164	Steel Building	151

Note: Average was QAR834 and Median QAR800.
Source: BRCA survey of Nepali workers in Qatar in 2005, and follow-up field work in 2009.

The Migration Process from Nepal to Qatar

One of the main characteristics of this corridor is that migration from Nepal to Qatar is managed in both countries. Managed migration is the norm in the Gulf region, unlike migration from Latin America to the United States or Africa to Western Europe. Nepali workers can leave Nepal only after their departure authorization is granted from the Department of Foreign Employment (DoFE). In Qatar, the Ministry of Labor regulates labor migration and the Ministry of Interior controls immigration processes. The two countries

Box 1.1. Skills Development Training among Nepali Migrant Workers

A few workers who came to Qatar as unskilled laborers have become accountants with training from their employers. There are also a few institutions in Qatar, which provide basic courses for migrant workers. These institutions usually focus on courses aimed at developing language and computer skills. A typical institution would train around 40–50 migrant workers a month from different nationalities and industries (such as construction, hotel, hospitality, and so forth). Migrant workers join such courses because they decide to develop their skills after arriving in Qatar, so as to obtain higher skilled jobs.

Source: BRCA fieldwork interviews

signed a manpower employment agreement in 2004 which aims to clarify migration procedures and accountability of key stakeholders. *Managed and temporary migration has resulted in Nepali migrants being documented workers in Qatar, which facilitates their access to formal financial institutions.*

Key Players in Nepal

The Department of Foreign Employment under the Ministry of Labor and Transport Management is responsible for the migration process and regulates Nepali manpower agencies. The Ministry of Labor has a labor attaché at the Embassy of Nepal in Qatar. The Foreign Employment Promotion Board was established under the Foreign Employment Act. Its responsibilities include promoting foreign employment, managing the Welfare Fund, monitoring manpower agencies and institutions for orientation and skill training, as well as formulating short- and long-term policies.

Recruitment (Manpower) agencies[8] play a key role in recruiting Nepali migrant workers and facilitating their migration process. Manpower agencies are required (under the FEA) to register with the Ministry of Labor and Transport Management.[9] These agencies often visit migrant-host countries to seek job opportunities for workers. In addition, there are many authorized training institutions that offer pre-departure training programs for migrants. These institutions are also required to register with the Ministry of Labor and Transport under the FEA.

Key Players in Qatar

Several Qatari ministries are responsible for managing migration to Qatar. The Ministry of Foreign Affairs coordinates with the Nepali government on migration policies and authenticates contracts.[10] According to the Labor Law of Qatar, the Ministry of Labor

Box 1.2. Terminology of Key Players in the Qatar-Nepal Migration Process

A *manpower agency* is a Nepali firm licensed to conduct recruitment of workers for foreign employment in Nepal. The agency may contract subagents who recruit workers at the local level on its behalf.

A *recruitment service company* is a Qatari firm licensed to conduct recruitment of foreign workers for a Qatari company (employer) that hires foreign workers.

A *middleman* is a generic term for a person or a company that provide services in the migration process. Services include recruitment of foreign workers or connecting the various concerned parties.

is responsible for: setting labor policies, deciding the proportion of non-Qatari workers, regulating employment of foreign workers, granting authorization for Qatari companies to hire foreign labor, as well as granting licenses to Qatari foreign employment recruitment services companies—and supervising these companies. The Ministry of Interior is responsible for the entry of migrant workers to Qatar, issuance of identification documents, and the maintenance of a national database.

Qatari companies hire foreign workers after receiving authorization from the Ministry of Labor. Recruitment service companies in their turn, provide foreign workers recruitment services for Qatari companies. There are also unregistered middlemen who illegally provide recruitment services to Qatari companies.

Steps of the Migration Process

A Qatari employer is required to obtain the Ministry of Labor's authorization to hire foreign workers. In the authorization, the company identifies the number of foreign workers to be hired and their nationalities. The employer is required to use a Qatari recruitment service company except in certain cases.[11] The recruitment service company (with the help of Nepali manpower agencies) identifies the Nepali workers and processes all migrant worker-related documents on behalf of the employer. In return, the employer pays a commission, travel expenses and other costs to the recruitment service company. Under the 2004 Bilateral Manpower Employment Agreement, the Qatari employer is required to bear all travel expenses of the workers from Nepal to the place of work in Qatar. Qatari recruitment service companies are also prohibited from receiving from the worker any recruitment fees, expenses or any other costs.[12]

Qatari recruitment service companies recruit workers in Nepal through Nepali manpower agencies. The Nepali manpower agencies identify the workers, complete all the required processing for the workers and seek authorization for them to depart Nepal for work migration. In order to obtain a Qatari visa, the agency sends copies of passports and signed contracts to the Qatari service company. Back in Qatar, the recruitment service company takes copies of passports and signed contracts to the Ministry of Labor for authorization and obtains a visa from the Ministry of Interior. After the Embassy of Nepal, the Qatari Chamber of Commerce or the Qatari Ministry of Foreign Affairs attest the contract, the Nepali Ministry of Foreign Employment authorizes the departure of migrant workers (see Chart 1.1 for a visual description of the whole migration process).

Pre-departure Orientation

Prior to departure, Nepali migrant workers are required by the Department of Foreign Employment to take orientation classes. These classes are run by licensed orientation companies. A certificate is presented upon completion of the classes. Workers learn about such things as geographical, cultural, social, political and economic conditions in destination countries, language, HIV/AIDS, communicative diseases, sexual and reproductive health, occupational safety and health, travel, treatment and security of workers, and repatriation of earnings made abroad to Nepal in a simple, easy and safe manner. Training on the use of formal remittance services is part of the orientation course.

There are approximately 40 licensed orientation companies under the Foreign Employment Act of 2007. According to the Ministry of Labor, these 40 companies are closely monitored by the authorities. Before the 2007 law was enacted, it was widely known that

Chart 1.1. The Nepal-Qatar Migration Process

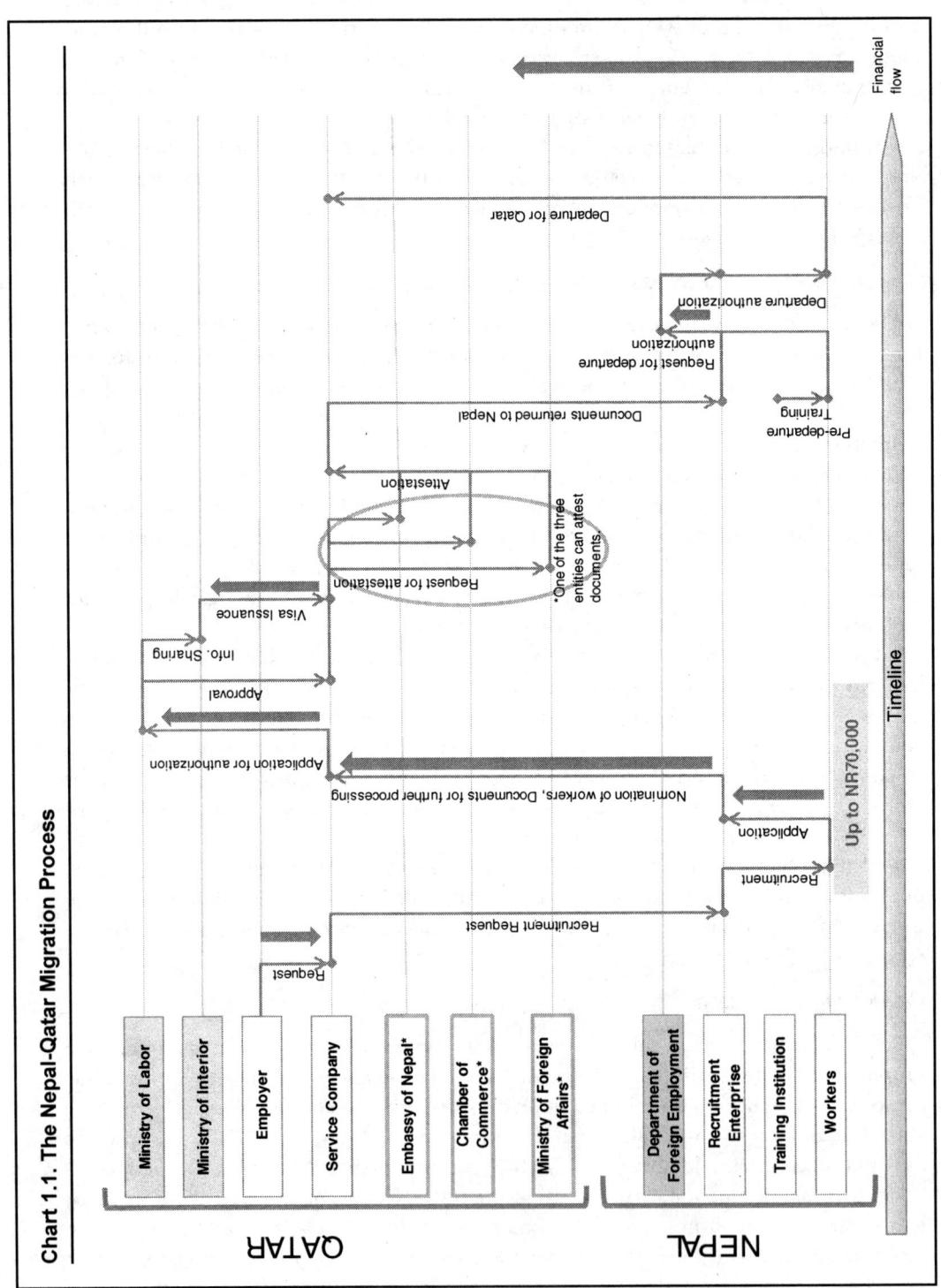

Source: Based on research and fieldwork

few migrant workers attended orientation classes and manpower agencies purchased the orientation certificates on behalf of the migrant workers. According to industry sources, this practice appears to continue (albeit on a much smaller scale), despite the new law.

Challenges in the Migration Process

There are many challenges in the migration process from Nepal to Qatar, which affect the integrity of remittance flows in this corridor. As explained in detail below, this is a result of the lack of enforcement of relevant regulations especially with respect to the roles played by manpower agencies in Nepal and recruitment service companies and (unlicensed) middlemen in Qatar.[13]

High Migration Costs

Nepali workers over-pay in migration fees to manpower agencies. The problem is caused by discrepancies between Qatari and Nepali regulations, lack of enforcement of these regulations and the bilateral agreement, as well as an unclear mix of legitimate and illegitimate fees. Lack of awareness among migrant workers exacerbates the problem.

Under the Foreign Employment Act of Nepal, Nepali manpower agencies are allowed to collect fees from migrants up to a certain designated amount. In the case of migration to Qatar, they are allowed to collect up to NPR70,000 (US$958) in overall fees from migrants. This ceiling is set based on the required fees and taxes, as well as an estimation of the necessary costs, expenses, and an appropriate level of profits for these agencies. As shown in figure 1.2 below, commissions to Qatari recruitment service company (or illegal middlemen) and air-fare expenses are estimated to be the two largest cost items, accounting for around 80 percent of the overall fee of NPR70,000:

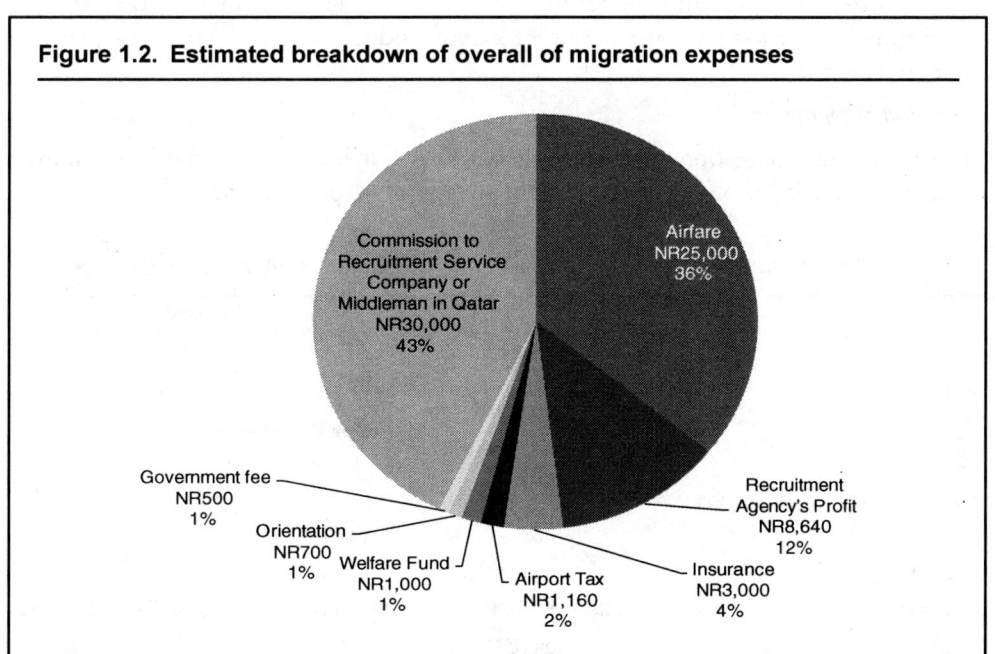

Figure 1.2. Estimated breakdown of overall of migration expenses

Commission to Recruitment Service Company or Middleman in Qatar
NR30,000
43%

Airfare
NR25,000
36%

Government fee
NR500
1%

Orientation
NR700
1%

Welfare Fund
NR1,000
1%

Airport Tax
NR1,160
2%

Insurance
NR3,000
4%

Recruitment Agency's Profit
NR8,640
12%

Source: Authors' calculation based on interviews.

On the other hand, Qatar's Labor Law prohibits commissions to recruitment service companies and the Qatar-Nepal bilateral agreement provides that all travel expenses are to be paid by the Qatari employer. The Labor Law in Qatar clearly stipulates that a recruitment service company is prohibited from "receiving from the worker any amount of money representing recruitment fees or expenses or any other costs."[14] This provision can be interpreted in such a way that these companies cannot receive any fees *directly* from the workers but can receive them from manpower agencies in other countries. However, the Ministry of Labor in Qatar has confirmed that such commissions are prohibited altogether. With regard to the air fare, Article 6 of the bilateral agreement clearly stipulates that the employer shall bear all travel expenses of the workers from Nepal to their place of work in Qatar upon entering the service for the first time, as well as the expenses of the return passage.

Actually, the combined officially required migration-related fees collected by Nepali and Qatari authorities do not exceed around US$465 (Table 1.4 below). Total officially required migration fees in Nepal add up to NPR6,360 (around US$87), whereas total fees collected by Qatar authorities in order to allow a migrant worker to enter the country and obtain a work permit amount to QAR1,375 (around US$378).

Therefore, there seem to be discrepancies and inconsistencies in the regulations, agreements, and practices governing migration expenses. Although Qatar's Labor Law prohibits payment of commissions, and the bilateral agreement stipulates that the employer should pay for travel expenses, the NPR70,000 ceiling set by the Nepali authorities does paradoxically allow Nepali manpower agencies to legally collect these costs from migrants. The weak enforcement of the bilateral agreement has also forced migrant workers to pay for costs and expenses which should be covered by an employer.

As a result of this, in practice, Nepali workers end up paying between US$395 to US$3,000 in total migration expense to Qatar, with an average payment of US$1,216.[15] This average is about 2.5 times larger than Nepal's GDP per capita in 2009 (US$470) and 4 to 6 times larger than a construction or service industry worker's average monthly salary in Qatar.[16]

Financing of Migration

In order to pay migration costs, Nepali workers borrow money from their family members and local moneylenders. A field survey of Nepali migrants in Qatar found

Table 1.4. Official migration fees levied in Nepal and Qatar as of June 2009

Nepal			Qatar		
	Amount			Amount	
Items	US$	NPR	Item	US$	QAR
Gov't fee for work permit		500	Visa submission fee		220
Life insurance		3,000	Medical fee		100
Contribution to foreign worker welfare fund		1,000	Visa fee		1,150
Orientation classes		700	ID card fee		50
Airport Tax		1,160			
Sub total	US$87.08	NPR6,360	Sub total	US$377.75	QAR1,375
		Total US$464.83			

Source: Nepal Department of Labor and Qatar Ministry of Labor.

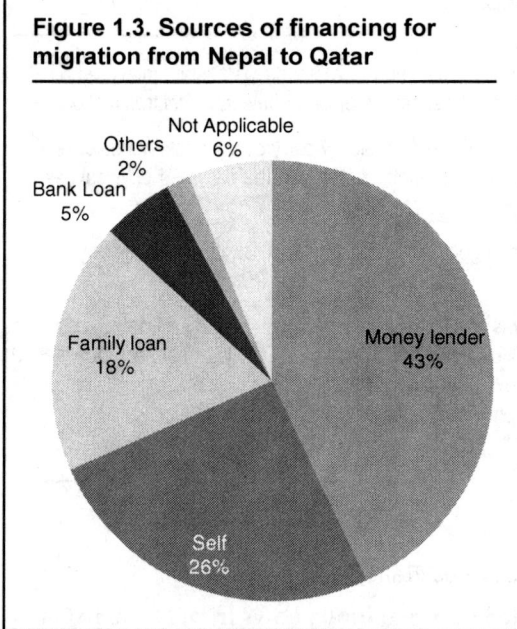

Figure 1.3. Sources of financing for migration from Nepal to Qatar

Not Applicable 6%
Others 2%
Bank Loan 5%
Family loan 18%
Money lender 43%
Self 26%

Source: Authors' questionnaire in Qatar.

that a bit less than half of the respondents relied on themselves or family members to cover their migration cost, whereas only a small fraction of these migrants availed of loans from formal financial institutions. Not surprisingly, 43 percent of the respondents used local moneylenders that charged high interest rates ranging from 24 to 36 percent .[17]

As a result, remittances sent by migrant workers during the first year are used to repay their migration loans, limiting the amount of remittances available for their families. With high interest rates (especially in the case of moneylenders), overall migration costs add-up to even higher than what migrants actually paid to migrate.

In order to address this problem, the Nepali government initiated schemes to provide incentives for financial institutions to provide migration loans. However, these programs have had limited success. One such scheme, which was eventually stopped, was launched by a consortium of Nepali banks around five years ago. It involved a tripartite agreement between the borrower (the migrant), banks and GON. The loan qualified as deprived sector lending and was insured by the government-owned Credit Guarantee Corporation up to (CGC) 75 percent of default amount. However, around 90 percent of the borrowers defaulted and the CGC ended up gradually repaying these loans (default typically started from the second month of the loan disbursement). The main reasons for default were the politically-motivated screening-process and the inexistence of agreements between the lending bank and employer's bank abroad to deduct part of the monthly salary for loan repayment. Another scheme, the Employment Development Bank has been operating in Nepal for a few years—with one of its main objectives being the financing of migration. However, the bank seems to be more involved in the real estate and retail/consumer lending sector and dedicates only a small part of its portfolio to finance migration because of the high risk (high default risk, no/poor collateral, high cost of funds) and low return involved in financing migration.

Too Many Middlemen

There appear to be many middlemen involved in the migration process. *These middlemen are not licensed in both countries.* There could be as many as three or four middlemen involved in different segments of migration process. These middlemen can be current or former migrant workers who are knowledgeable of labor market conditions and can connect a Qatari recruitment service company with Nepali manpower agencies. The involvement of many middlemen clouds procedures and generates additional fees.

Box 1.3. Types of IFT Systems in South Asia

In South Asia, a variety of simple as well as quite sophisticated informal methods to transfer funds exist. The main three methods are: courier services, in-kind remittances, and the use of *hawala/hundi* transactions.

Courier services are the simplest way of moving funds. People physically carry cash or ask friends or relatives to carry them. However, courier services are risky and inefficient due to the nature of physical cash transfer.

In-kind remittances take place through the provision of goods or services in one country, while the payment is made in another country.

Finally, a typical *hawala/hundi* transaction involves the remitter, the recipient, and two intermediaries (*hawaladars*). The remitter makes payment in local currency in a sending country to the service provider. The service provider contacts a partner service provider in a receiving country, who arranges payment in local currency to the recipient in exchange for reference code that was given to the remitter by the provider in the sending country.

Source: Authors' fieldwork in select countries.

Transfers of Commissions[18] through Informal Funds Transfer (IFT) Systems

The current migration process has prompted informal funds flows from Nepal to Qatar, in order to transfer the commissions of middlemen and recruitment service companies. While most of the remittance flows in this corridor are from Qatar to Nepal, it is important to highlight that the commissions of Qatari recruitment service companies flow in the other direction through IFT methods (the *Hundi*—see Box 1.3).

On the Nepali side, Nepali manpower agencies use Hundi to transfer these commissions for several reasons. First, by using Hundi, manpower agencies in Nepal can avoid leaving a paper trail and therefore avoid paying the required Tax Deductions at the Payment Source (TDS), when they send commissions. Although Nepali authorities reduced the TDS gradually from 15 percent to 5 percent to address this problem, all commissions from Nepal to Qatar are still being paid through informal channels. Second, given that the NRB imposes restrictions on capital outflows from Nepal (and requires approval of this type of transfer on case-by-case individual basis), Nepali manpower agencies prefer using IFT methods.

On the Qatari side, as discussed earlier, commissions to recruitment service companies are prohibited. Therefore, Qatari recruitment service companies prefer to receive these commissions through informal methods without leaving payment records. In addition, unlicensed or unauthorized middlemen providing migrant recruitment services in Qatar avoid receiving their fees and commissions through formal channels.

The amount of commissions transferred from Nepal to Qatar is estimated to range from US$17 million to US$34 million per annum.[19] In general, a manpower agency pays US$250 to US$500 per migrant as commissions to a recruitment service company in Qatar. Commissions are paid in approximately 80 percent of migration transactions. In 2007/08, 84,000 workers went to Qatar. These reverse flows amount to around 5 percent of recorded remittance flows from Qatar to Nepal.

Notes

1. GCC member states are Bahrain, Kuwait, Oman, Qatar, Saudi Arabia, and the United Arab Emirates.

2. IOM and Economist Intelligence Unit (EIU) estimates.

3. Global Economic Prospects Group, World Bank data for all; IMF data for UAE; and QCB data for Qatar.

4. In July 2008, the Government of Qatar developed "Qatar National Vision 2030", which is a comprehensive development plan that "aims at transforming Qatar into an advanced country by 2030." The National Vision has four pillars: human development, social development, diversified economic development and environmental development.

5. Ministry of Labor, Qatar.

6. QAR500–800.

7. QAR1,000–2,500.

8. There are about 700 recruitment firms in Nepal, operating under the supervision of the Department of Foreign Employment. Around 400 companies belong to the National Association of Foreign Employment Agencies (NAFEA), see www.nafea.org/aboutus.php.

9. Requirements for registration include: 1) Bank guarantee of NPR3 million (US$41,073), or 2) a bank guarantee of NPR2,300,000 ($31,490) and cash deposit of NPR700,000 (US$9,583) to obtain a license.

10. Authentication is done by the Ministry of Foreign Affairs of Qatar, the Embassy of Nepal in Qatar, and the Chamber of Commerce in Qatar.

11. The employer may not recruit workers from abroad except through a person or entity authorized to do so. An exception to this provision is that the employer or his authorized representative may recruit workers from abroad for his own account after obtaining the approval of the Ministry. This approval is not required if the employer is a household.

12. Article (33), Labor Law (Qatar).

13. Although Nepali workers can independently migrate abroad, the majority continue to count on the services of manpower without being prepared with knowledge and information of the migration process

14. Article 33, Qatar Labor Law.

15. Survey of Nepali migrant workers in Qatar. The average cost is NPR91,616.

16. Since these malpractices are widespread regionally, addressing them bilaterally between Qatar and Nepal may make Nepal less attractive as an origination of migrant workers. Thus, it may be necessary to address these issues on regional level.

17. Responses were collected through a survey of 105 Nepali workers in different locations in Qatar.

18. A commission as referred to in this report specifically means money paid by Nepali recruitment agencies to Qatari employment service companies and/or Qatari employers in exchange for employment contracts.

19. World Bank fieldwork and author calculations: 80 percent of 84000 migrants * US$250 per migrant as commission (low-end total commission of US$17million); 80 percent of 84000 migrants * US$500 (high-end total commission of US$34million)

CHAPTER 2

The Remittance Transfer Process

This chapter discusses the overall remittance transfer process from Qatar to Nepal and attempts to answer the following questions:

▪ *What is the size and trend of remittance outflows from Qatar?*
▪ *What is the size and significance of remittance inflows to Nepal?*
▪ *What about remittance flows from Qatar and Nepal?*
▪ *What are the characteristics and key features of the remittance market landscape in both Qatar and Nepal?*
▪ *What are some of the challenges underlying the remittance transfer process from Qatar to Nepal?*

Total Remittance Outflows, Destinations and Trends from Qatar

Remittance outflows from Qatar surpassed US$8.98 billion in 2009 (around 10.7 percent of real GDP),[1] up from US$1.9 billion in 2002—an increase of 373 percent in seven years (Figure 2.1). As discussed earlier, the main reason for the growth of remittance outflows is the consistent growth of Qatar's economy and the ensuing high demand for foreign workers. Many of these workers remit money regularly back home.

Remittance flows to Nepal account for 7 percent of the total outflows from Qatar. The main destinations of remittance outflows from Qatar are Asian countries (account-

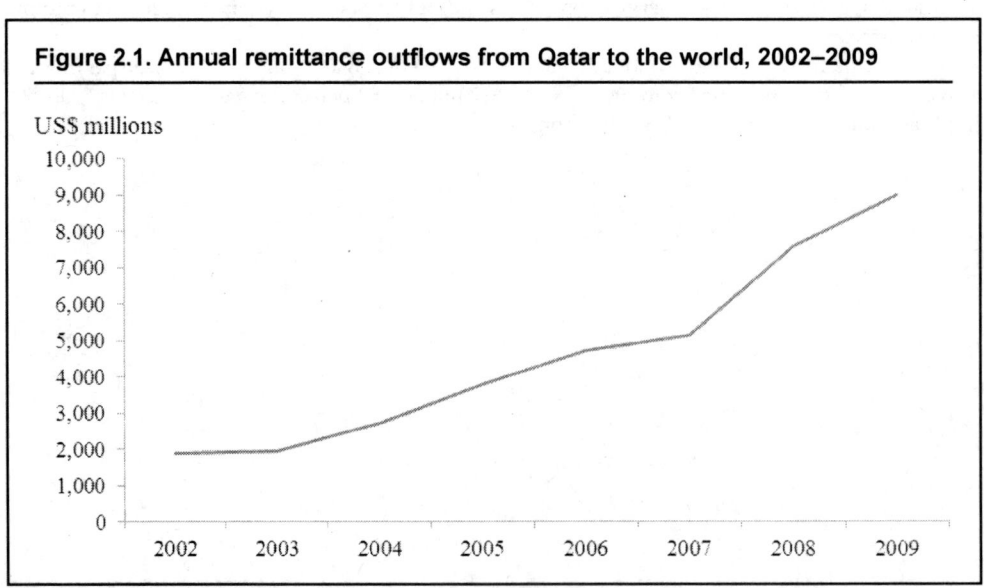

Figure 2.1. Annual remittance outflows from Qatar to the world, 2002–2009

US$ millions

Source: Qatar Central Bank.

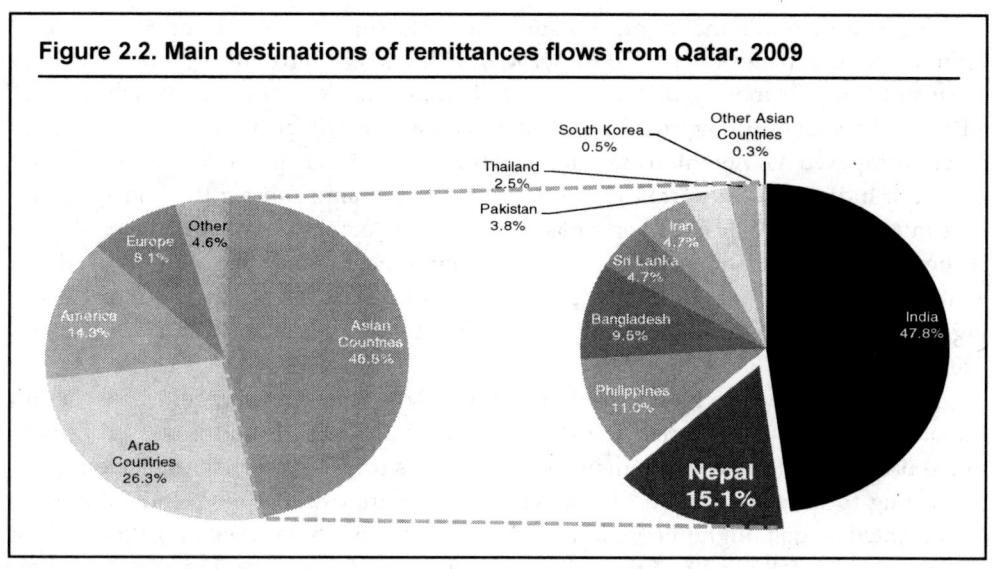

Figure 2.2. Main destinations of remittances flows from Qatar, 2009

Source: Qatar Central Bank.

ing for 47 percent of these flows in 2009), followed by Arab countries (with a share of 26 percent)—see Figure 2.2. Among Asian countries, India is the largest destination, while Nepal accounted for some 15 percent of remittance outflows to Asian countries and 7 percent of worldwide remittance outflows from Qatar.

Total Remittance Inflows to Nepal and their Significance

Remittances have been playing a major role in Nepal's economy over the past decade, rising from less than US$100 million in Fiscal Year (FY) 2000 to US$2.7 billion in FY 2008–09 or 21.8 percent of GDP.[2] This has made Nepal the ninth largest remittance receiving country in the world as a percentage of its GDP (Figure 2.3) and the largest in South Asia. Remittances are also the largest source of foreign exchange in Nepal and have helped offset the country's deteriorating trade deficit since 2001.

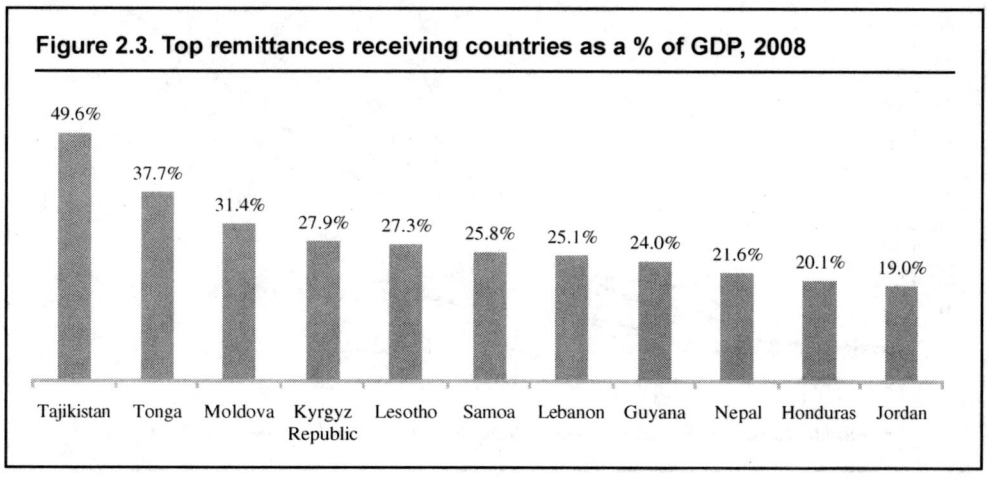

Figure 2.3. Top remittances receiving countries as a % of GDP, 2008

Source: World Bank.

The rise in remittances comes against a backdrop of a less impressive overall economic performance over the past decade, with real GDP growth averaging around 4 percent.[3] This is mainly due to civil conflict and political uncertainty which have left Nepal's economy lagging behind South Asia's recent growth boom, especially when compared to neighboring India (Nepal's real GDP growth was about half of that of India the past decade). Therefore, Nepal remains among the poorest countries in Asia. Nevertheless, poverty has continued to decrease—and with an estimated 30 percent of Nepali households receiving remittances, the latter were singled out as the main factor contributing to the reduction in the share of the population living in poverty from 42 percent to 31 percent between 1996 and 2004 (World Bank, 2006).

Remittance flows to Nepal originate mainly from the Gulf region, Malaysia and India. Nepali migration started to gather pace in the late 1990s and increased rapidly in the past half a decade. More than 200,000 Nepalis travel to work abroad every year. According to the Department of Foreign Employment, there are around 1.3 million documented Nepali migrants. Excluding India, Malaysia is the primary host country for Nepali workers, followed by Qatar, Saudi Arabia, and United Arab Emirates (see chart below). Estimates of Nepalis working in India vary between one to two million (most of whom are undocumented).

While remittance flows to Nepal grew by an annual average of 39 percent between FY07 and FY09, the growth rate slowed down to 11 percent in the first six months of FY10. The global financial crisis affected the slowdown in many ways, such as: slower increase in the stock of migrants (migrant departures declined by 5 percent in FY09, and increased by 10 percent in the first six months of FY10); worsening employment and wage situation in some destination economies; and exchange rate movements (Figure 2.5).

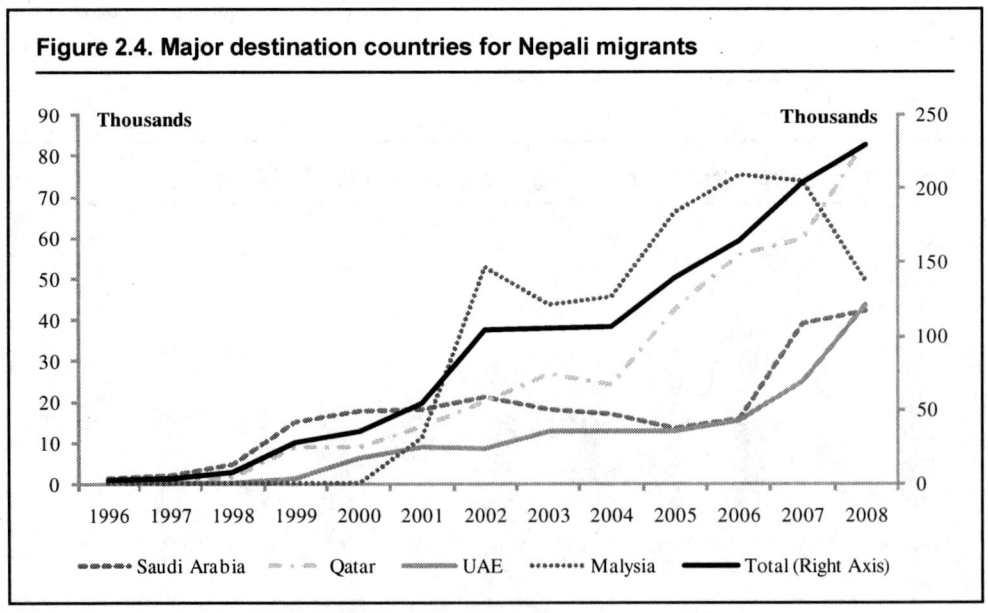

Figure 2.4. Major destination countries for Nepali migrants

Source: Department of Foreign Employment (DoFE)—Government of Nepal.

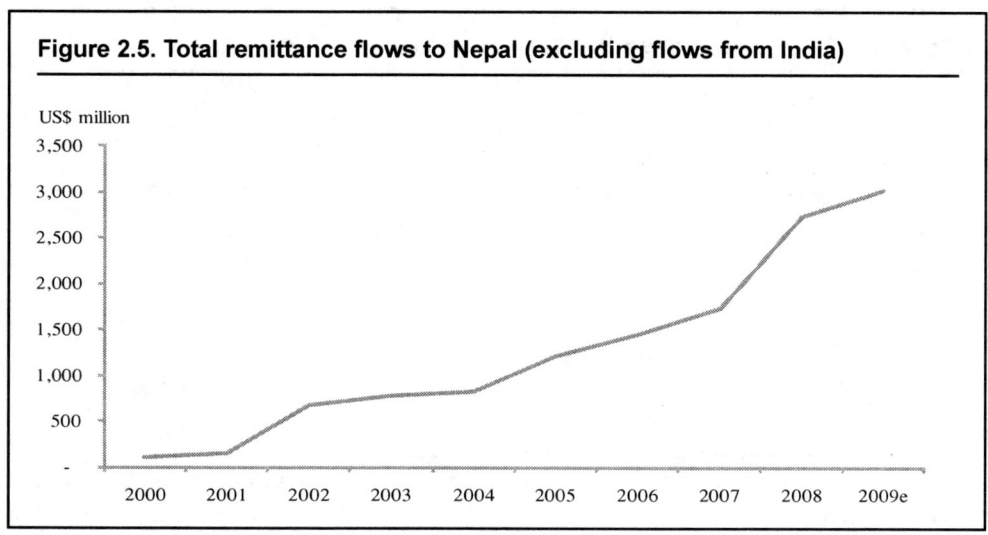

Figure 2.5. Total remittance flows to Nepal (excluding flows from India)

Source: NRB and World Bank

Remittance Flows between Qatar and Nepal

Remittance flows from Qatar to Nepal surpassed US$634 million in 2009 (or around 21 percent of Nepal's overall remittance inflows in 2009). These flows have continued to grow especially since 2004, driven by the increase in Nepali workers' migration to Qatar and the gradual shift from informal to formal channels. The spectacular growth from 2004 to 2006 (of more than 100 percent per year) is explained by the large construction boom, mainly in preparation for the 15th Asian Games in Doha.

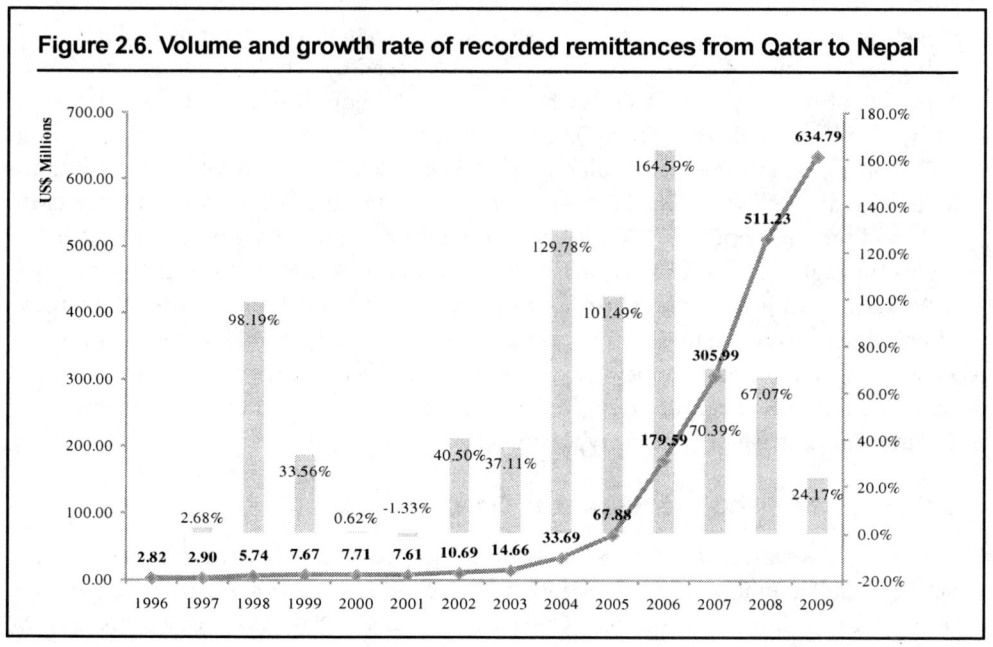

Figure 2.6. Volume and growth rate of recorded remittances from Qatar to Nepal

Source: Qatar Central Bank.

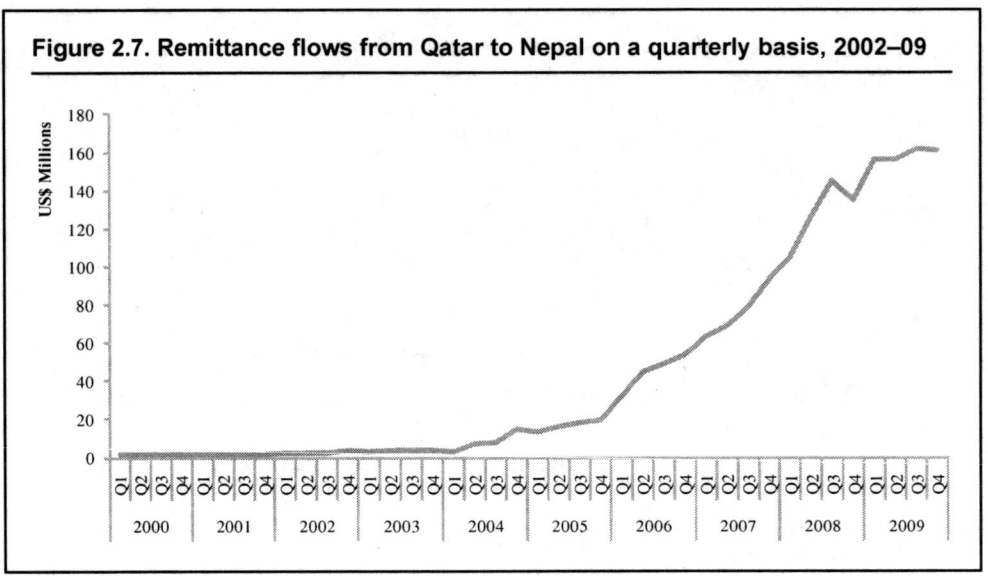

Figure 2.7. Remittance flows from Qatar to Nepal on a quarterly basis, 2002–09

Source: Qatar Central Bank.

The slower growth rate in remittances in 2008 and 2009 (including a drop in absolute remittance flows in the fourth quarter of 2008) could be attributed to the negative impact of the global financial crisis. While the number of Nepali migrant workers in Qatar continued to increase between 2007 and 2009, the growth rate was lower than in previous years.

Despite the exponential growth of remittance flows from Qatar to Nepal since 2004, one clear pattern persists, which is that while Nepali migrants in Qatar constituted around a quarter of the migrant workforce in 2008, they sent to Nepal only 7 percent of the overall remittance outflows from Qatar. The reasons for this under-remitting could be the lower wages that Nepali workers receive on average and the continued, albeit small and diminishing, use of informal channels (as evidenced by the fact that the transfers of commissions from Nepal to Qatar have to be offset by equivalent amounts of informal workers' remittances flowing from Qatar to Nepal).

This phenomenon has led Nepali migrant workers to engage in a collective remittance scheme known as *Dhikuti*. *Dhikuti* traditionally operates as a loan system among close friends and families, and it is used by Nepali workers with the lowest salaries. *Dhikuti* operates through a group of four or five trusted friends and/or family members. Each month, a different group member collects money from the others in order to increase the total transfer amount to his family. This way, each group member's family in Nepal receives a larger amount of money once every four or five months giving them additional options for the use of remittances. It also reduces remittance transfer costs since the remittance transfer fee in Qatar is typically a fixed fee.

The Remittance Market Landscape in Qatar

Recent years have witnessed a surge in the number of remittance market players in Qatar, which has resulted in increasing competition, thereby significantly reducing average prices for remittance services in the corridor.[4] One reason for this is Qatar's well-development payment systems infrastructure. Qatar's payment system includes a SWIFT-based Real-Time

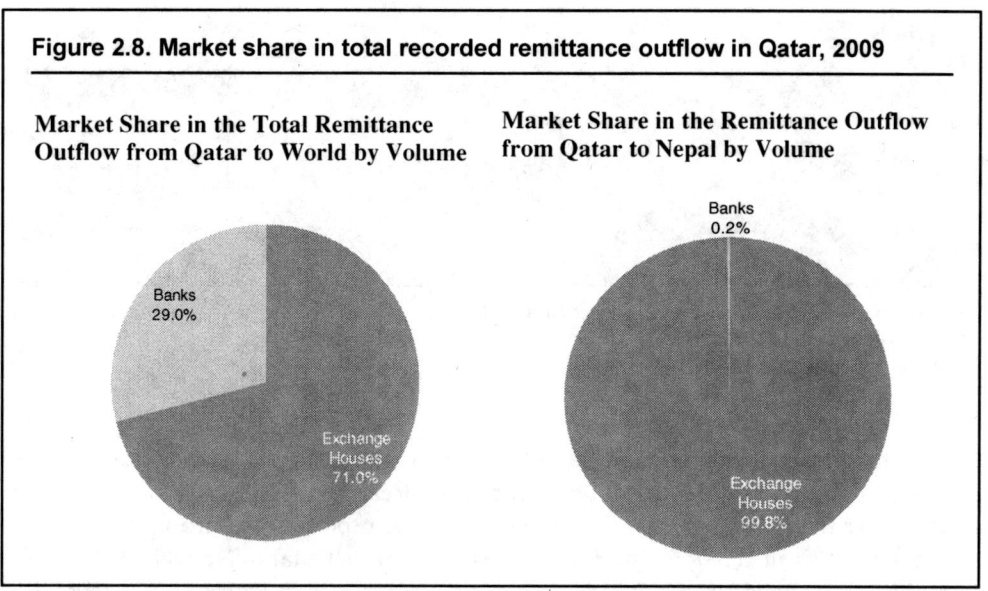

Figure 2.8. Market share in total recorded remittance outflow in Qatar, 2009

Market Share in the Total Remittance Outflow from Qatar to World by Volume

Market Share in the Remittance Outflow from Qatar to Nepal by Volume

Banks 29.0%

Exchange Houses 71.0%

Banks 0.2%

Exchange Houses 99.8%

Source: Qatar Central Bank.

Gross Settlement (RTGS) system that is linked to the QCB's clearing system, the Government's securities system, and the currency issuing application. Qatar also has a National ATM and POS Switch (NAPS), which is an interface that hosts and settles all local retail electronic transactions flowing between local banks.

In Qatar, remittance service providers are exchange houses, banks, and the postal service. However, exchange houses play a leading role, particularly in the Qatar-Nepal remittance corridor, where they account for 99.8 percent of market share. The key players are Habib Exchange, Al-Fardan Exchange, National Exchange, and Doha Bank.

Exchange Houses (MTOs)

Exchange houses serve as money transfer operators themselves and/or as agents of Western Union. There are twenty licensed exchange houses in Qatar, with a total of forty operating branches and five additional branches having received approval from QCB. Until recently, exchange houses were only permitted to have a maximum of two branches in addition to their main office but this provision has been changed. QCB now decides the number of branches based on its assessment of demand for their services. Currently, three exchange houses have more than four branches in operation.

The large increase in the number of Nepali workers in Qatar encouraged more exchange houses to provide remittance services for the Qatar-Nepal remittance corridor. In 1995, only one exchange house provided remittance services to Nepal. By 2005, this number had risen to 10, while at the end of 2009, all exchange houses in Qatar offered remittance services in the Qatar-Nepal corridor. Exchange houses in Qatar have hosted staff of Nepali financial institutions for the purposes of marketing and promoting remittance products. These Nepali employees are able to communicate with Nepali customers in their own language and can also approach migrant workers outside the office by visiting workers' camps to market remittance products and gather feedback from migrant workers.

Nepalese workers line up for their turns to send remittances at an exchange house on a Friday evening. (Photo: Isaku Endo)

Banks

Most of the 18 banks[5] operating in Qatar do not view remittances as an attractive product or an entry point for marketing other financial services. As a result, most banks in Qatar do not offer their own individual remittance service products. According to the QCB, only three banks engaged in remittance transactions from Qatar to Nepal in 2009.[6] Doha Bank has been the leading bank in the remittance business in Qatar: it has developed an internet-based account-to-account remittance service which is priced relatively competitively, and it offers short message services (SMS) to a remitter for the confirmation of remittance delivery. In addition, it has pioneered Mobile Banking Units, which are vehicles that carry bank staff and an ATM to locations where Nepali migrant workers live or work, and provides them with access to a whole range of banking services. To date, it operated three such units. Doha Bank is also an agent of Western Union.

Postal Service

The Qatar Postal Corporation (Q-Post) offers money order services to twenty one countries including Nepal. Q-Post is also an agent of Western Union. Q-Post started money order services to and from Nepal (through an agreement with Nepal Post) in February 2004. *Although the fee for sending remittances through money order is QAR10 per QAR1,000 sent (which is lower than the fees charged by Qatari exchange houses and banks), no money order has been issued from Qatar to Nepal since the service began.* This is because of the slower speed of money orders, the ceiling on the maximum remittance amount through money orders (US$2,000), the inconvenient office hours, and the language barrier.

Informal Transfers in Qatar

The use of informal channels to send remittances from Qatar to Nepal has declined sharply over the past decade. Before 2001, most Nepali migrant workers used these channels largely because of the high cost, lower speed and limited availability of formal remittance channels. However, informal transfer mechanisms rapidly lost popularity in this corridor due to fraud, malpractice, transfer delays, as well as increased awareness about formal channels, their increased availability and decreasing costs. According to the BRCA field survey, only 3 percent of Nepali migrants used *Hundi*.

Declining Role of International MTOs in the Qatar Nepal Corridor

Given the fierce competition in the Qatari market, international MTOs such as Western Union and Money Gram have both seen a gradual decline in their market share and profit margins. This has compelled MoneyGram to exit Qatar's market altogether and has forced Western Union to focus their operations on other countries that have greater potential such as Saudi Arabia, Kuwait, Oman, and Lebanon. Doha Bank and exchange houses (with partner entities on the Nepali side) typically charge lower prices than international MTOs by sending money through their own individual remittance network, and their services tend to be customized to the needs and requirements of Nepali workers. In addition, their services are as fast and secure as those offered by the International MTOs.

The Remittance Market Landscape in Nepal

The remittance market in Nepal is relatively well-developed, with a number of banks, money transfer operators (MTOs) and other institutions providing remittance services. According to Nepal Rastra Bank, 20 private commercial banks, 3 state-owned banks, 4 finance companies, 12 micro-finance institutions, Nepal Post, as well as 47 non-banking entities are authorized to receive and deliver remittances. Some of these local non-bank entities are principal agents of international MTOs. Non-bank RSPs are licensed by NRB. International MTOs are currently not required to apply for a separate RSP license since their principal agents are required to be licensed.

NRB estimates that the combined market share of the non-bank RSP's and international MTOs is around 70 percent, with banks accounting for the remaining 30 percent market share. The market is dominated by two large non-bank RSPs and one bank. Except for a few large commercial banks, most banks are very insignificant players in the remittances market. The share of Western Union is estimated to be around 10–15 percent, and it is the largest international MTO in Nepal. In addition there are community based arrangements, such as physical transportation of cash and *hundi*, which process remittances. These arrangements are estimated to process an additional 20–30 percent of the remittances processed by RSPs, mostly from India. Mobile phone operators in Nepal are not authorized to send or receive remittances.

From an end-to-end perspective, the remittance market in Nepal is mainly cash to cash. Around 90 percent of the recipients receive payments in cash, while the remainder receives payments into their accounts with banks/financial institutions. The cash-to-cash remittances are usually "instant" transfers (the recipient can technically collect cash from the RSPs agent in Nepal right after the sender completes the transaction in the sending country). In general, the recipients collect cash within the same day with almost all collected within 3 days. The Credit-to-Account remittances processing is usually within one day if the recipient maintains bank account in a designated bank. Recipients having accounts in other banks, would face a wait-time of up to 10 days depending on where the recipient has his account, as the check needs to be sent to that bank through post or by courier and would then need to be cleared by his bank.

Money Transfer Operators (MTOs)

International money transfer operators, such as Western Union and MoneyGram, along with local Nepali money transfer operators (such as Prabhu and IME), dominate the remittance market in Nepal. International money transfer operators have their own agent network that comprises of commercial banks, local money transfer companies and other companies. Local MTOs such as International Money Express (IME) and Prabhu Money Transfer have engaged in remittance transactions from various countries in the Gulf region and Malaysia. In total, non-bank MTOs have over 2,500 branches across the country.

While the international money transfer operators tend to enforce exclusivity agreements on their agent network, national money transfer operators tend to specialize in the main remittance corridors—such as the Gulf region and Malaysia—to Nepal and have branched out even in remote areas across the country where payments may arrive in the same day or the next. This occurs through a system of agents; these agents only need to obtain a Money Transfer license from NRB and electricity/telephone/fax connections. Should an agent not have internet, he/she will simply contact the head office (with a toll free number), which will process the transaction on the agent's behalf.

Some MTO's have developed partnerships with foreign banks or MTOs to develop the remittance network, including in Qatar. For example, Arabian Exchange Company in Qatar has a partnership with Nepal Bank and Prabhu Money Transfer in Nepal to deliver remittances. In addition, some Nepali MTOs have partnered with microfinance development banks and finance companies and a few have begun to offer foreign employment loans (either group or collateral guaranteed), deposit accounts, debit cards and checking accounts to Nepali migrants. Nepali migrant workers are able to open such accounts abroad and wire remittances directly into them. International Money Express offers direct deposits to bank accounts in Nepal, with the money transferred immediately to the partner IME Financial Institution Limited, while it takes longer to reach other banks. With increasingly large volumes of remittances, MTO's have discovered the need to develop liquidity management mechanisms and hedging products.

NRB has created an incentive for MTOs to engage in the remittance business (with the aim of increasing market competition and discouraging MTOs from engaging in underground activity) by allowing MTOs to sell their foreign exchange (or dollars received from remittance inflows) to commercial banks or to NRB at more favorable exchange rates. MTOs now receive NPR15 paisa additional benefit for every US$1 for selling their foreign exchange directly with NRB. However, this scheme does not seem to be used very often, except when there is a shortage of foreign exchange in the market-since banks seem to compete for the foreign exchange of MTO's (especially large ones) and thus provide these MTOs with favorable FX rates.

Banks

Despite the large remittance market only a few Nepali Banks have entered this market. Most of them offer basic remittance services through bank-to-bank SWIFT transfers or bank drafts. Some banks serve as agents of international MTOs. Other banks, such as Himalayan Bank (the leading bank in the remittance market) have developed their own proprietary software (Himalremit, which is web-based). Many banks are not active in this market because all the remittances are anyway indirectly channeled through the bank, as the non-bank RSP needs to convert the amount collected in foreign currency to Nepali rupees for disbursement in Nepal through banks, where they are able to enjoy the foreign exchange commission. Also some banks perceive managing agent networks as expensive. In order to enter the Qatari market, some Nepali banks have developed partnerships with Qatari banks or exchange houses. Such arrangements allow for speedier transfer of funds from Qatar to Nepal, than resorting to regular wire transfers through correspondent banking arrangements. An example of such partnerships is an arrangement between Habib Exchange in Qatar and Himalayan Bank in Nepal.

Postal Service

Nepal Post provides remittance services in the form of paper-based money orders as well as electronic money transfers (as one of the principal agents of Western Union). Nepal Post also has tie-ups with the Postal authorities of India, Hong Kong, Thailand, Qatar,

UAE and Jordan for receiving incoming international money orders. It is has a large network of office (521 of which are equipped to handle money orders, 117 of which offer Postal Banking). Currently Nepal Post is a marginal player in the remittances market. It processes incoming remittances of around US$1 million, almost all of it from India. As of March 2010, it had not yet received any remittances from Qatar. Its small market share is due to lack of resources, no automation, slower speed of sending remittances through money orders, and security concerns. Nepal Post has been making losses over the past few years, limiting its ability to invest in new technology and services.

Informal Transfers in Nepal

Remittance flows through informal transfer primarily originate from India, whose proximity, porous border and regulatory constraints are conducive to facilitating such flows. Nepalis do not require a visa to enter India, but in order to transfer remittances to Nepal, MTOs must route them through the Reserve Bank of India's approved banks, and the sender has to have proper documentation. This along with the relatively higher cost of formal remittance transfers, senders' lack of valid ID's, recipients' lack of access to a nearby bank branch or bank accounts, and mistrust/lack of information about electronic transfers all contribute to continued use of informal transfers.

Remittances through Mobile Phones

Current regulations in this corridor do not support the use of mobile phones for the transmission of cross-border remittances. However, banks and telecom companies are showing growing interest in this area. In Qatar, Doha Bank has received approval from QCB in May 2010 to pilot a project on mobile remittances with telecom operator Vodafone Qatar.[7] Vodafone's main competitor, Q-Tel, is also preparing to launch mobile phone remittance schemes between Qatar and some South Asian countries. In Nepal, a few banks, such as Bank of Kathmandu and Laxmi Bank, have already developed limited mobile banking applications, including sending and receiving money between customers of the same bank, and mobile phone-based payment services. However, the lack of proper NRB guidelines and unavailability of USSD platform[8] by the mobile phone operators (NT and Ncell) is slowing down further developments.

Globally, a few cross-border remittance schemes through mobile phones such as G-Cash in the Philippines and M-Pesa in Kenya have been successful because they provide lower transaction costs, expanded distribution networks, enhanced speed and security of the transactions and other convenience factors (such as being able to make transactions from anywhere). In addition, infrastructure costs are relatively not high and technological solutions are available off-the-shelf. In the context of Nepal, the use of mobile phones for financial transactions could expand access to financial services in remote and rural areas.

Remittance Transfer Fees between Qatar and Nepal

Because of the increased competition in both the Nepali and Qatar remittance markets, the fees for sending remittances from Qatar to Nepal have decreased by about fifty percent over since 2001. In 2001, most RSPs charged an average fee of QAR35, while Western Union charged 10 percent of the amount transferred. By 2005, the average remittance transfer fee declined by about 49 percent to QAR15 to 18, and has remained at that level ever since then. *It is important to note that the enactment of AML laws (in 2002/2003 in Qatar and 2008 in Nepal) did not affect the downward trend in the price of remittances in the corridor.*

Transfer fees are very competitive in the Qatar-Nepal remittance corridor, with an average cost of 3.41 percent for a US$200 remittance transfer (2.89 percent for the fee + 0.52 percent for forex margin). This compares favorably to the global average price of a US$200 remittance transfer, was 8.83 percent in the first quarter of 2010 (according to the World Bank's global remittance prices database which covers 178 remittance corridors). Table 2.1 shows remittance transfer prices charged by major Exchange Houses in Qatar (taking into account exchange rate margins).

Challenges for Remittance Transfers in the Qatar-Nepal Corridor

Limited RSP Coverage Outside Doha

Although RSPs in Qatar can now establish more than two branches (in addition to their main office), the new regulations have only recently taken effect and thus there remains limited RSP coverage outside Doha. Most Nepali migrant workers still feel compelled to travel to Doha to send remittances. Some migrant workers live near oil mining locations, where they do not have access to any formal remittance service providers, therefore, some of their employers arrange a bus service for them to travel to Doha during their free time on Fridays (the weekend). However, commercial banks are closed on Fridays, and exchange houses are only open for limited hours.

Limited Enthusiasm Among Qatari Commercial Banks to Enter Remittance Market

While commercial banks have expanded their branch network throughout the country recently, they have not engaged in the remittance business as much as exchange houses. In general, Qatari banks do not have incentives to enter the remittance market because they believe that remittance services are less profitable than their other services. With the exception of *Doha bank,* which is a retail-oriented bank, most Qatari banks are focused on corporate lending and do not have incentives to develop banking products for migrants. Since the services offered by exchange houses are cash-based services, this means that many Nepali migrant workers (especially those un/semi-skilled workers) do not have the opportunity to access savings accounts, which could provide them with safety and enable them access to other financial services.

Limited Development of the Domestic Payment Systems Infrastructure in Nepal

Another key challenge to transfer remittances in this corridor is the continuing constraints on the distribution of remittances at the receiving end. Most RSPs in Nepal continue to operate in Kathmandu and the surrounding areas, with limited presence in rural areas. One of the key reasons for this is Nepal's underdeveloped payment systems infrastructure. Nepal is largely a cash-based economy and there is no electronic funds transfer network for interbank payments. Checks are cleared manually. Interregional clearing can take up to 7 days, as the check has to be physically exchanged. For cross-border retail payments, correspondent banking arrangements are usually used. As a result, around 90 percent of the total remittances are Cash-Payout remittances. The low level of banking penetration among recipients and lack of awareness exacerbates the problem. This has led RSPs to maintain large agent networks to pay cash. In general an agent is paid around NPR100 per remittance. For certain large agents, RSPs have to prefund the agent to ensure they do not run out of cash. All this adds to the cost of processing remittances, which has a bearing on the remittance price paid by the sender.

The domestic payment infrastructure in Nepal is used for the transfer of funds within Nepal to agents for reimbursing prior cash disbursements to recipients. RSPs

Table 2.1. Remittance transfer prices from Qatar to Nepal, 2009

Exchange House	$100 or QAR364			$200 or QAR728			$500 or QAR1,820				
	Transfer Fee			Transfer Fee			Transfer Fee				
	QAR (US$)	Percent (%)	QAR (US$)	QAR (US$)	Percent (%)	QAR (US$)	QAR (US$)	Percent (%)	QAR (US$)	FX* Charged	FX Margin* (%)
Doha Exchange Company	15 (4.12)	4.45%	16.20 (4.45)	15 (4.12)	2.39%	17.4 (4.78)	15 (4.12)	1.15%	20.93 (5.75)	21.82	0.33%
Al Fardan Exchange Company	15 (4.12)	4.54%	16.53 (4.54)	15 (4.12)	2.48%	18.05 (4.96)	15 (4.12)	1.24%	22.56 (6.20)	21.80	0.42%
Islamic Exchange Company	18 (4.95)	5.15%	18.75 (5.15)	18 (4.95)	2.67%	19.44 (5.34)	18 (4.95)	1.19%	21.66 (5.95)	21.85	0.20%
Trust Exchange Company	18 (4.95)	5.19%	18.89 (5.19)	18 (4.95)	2.71%	19.73 (5.42)	18 (4.95)	1.23%	22.39 (6.15)	21.84	0.24%
Union Exchange Company	18 (4.95)	5.19%	18.89 (5.19)	18 (4.95)	2.71%	19.73 (5.42)	18 (4.95)	1.23%	22.39 (6.15)	21.84	0.24%
Al Dar for Exchange Works	18 (4.95)	5.24%	19.07 (5.24)	18 (4.95)	2.76%	20.09 (5.52)	18 (4.95)	1.28%	23.30 (6.40)	21.83	0.29%
Qatar-UAE Exchange	18 (4.95)	5.24%	19.07 (5.24)	18 (4.95)	2.76%	20.09 (5.52)	18 (4.95)	1.28%	23.30 (6.40)	21.83	0.29%
Arabian Exchange Company	18 (4.95)	5.24%	19.07 (5.24)	18 (4.95)	2.76%	20.09 (5.52)	18 (4.95)	1.28%	23.30 (6.40)	21.83	0.29%
City Exchange Company	18 (4.95)	5.24%	19.07 (5.24)	18 (4.95)	2.76%	20.09 (5.52)	18 (4.95)	1.28%	23.30 (6.40)	21.83	0.29%
Habib Qatar International Exchange Ltd	18 (4.95)	5.24%	19.07 (5.24)	18 (4.95)	2.76%	20.09 (5.52)	18 (4.95)	1.28%	23.30 (6.40)	21.83	0.29%
Al Mana Exchange Company	15 (4.12)	5.32%	19.36 (5.31)	15 (4.12)	3.26%	23.73 (6.52)	15 (4.12)	2.02%	36.76 (10.10)	21.63	1.20%
Al Sadd Exchange Company	20 (5.49)	6.19%	22.53 (6.19)	20 (5.49)	3.45%	25.12 (6.90)	20 (5.49)	1.79%	32.58 (8.95)	21.74	0.70%
Eastern Exchange Est	15 (4.12)	6.14%	22.35 (6.14)	15 (4.12)	4.08%	29.7 (8.16)	15 (4.12)	2.84%	51.69 (14.20)	21.45	2.02%
Average	**17.23 (4.73)**	**5.26%**	**19.14 (5.26)**	**17.23 (4.73)**	**2.89%**	**21.03 (5.78)**	**17.23 (4.73)**	**1.47%**	**26.73 (7.34)**	**21.78**	**0.52%**

Note: FER is denoted as Foreign Exchange Rate. Estimates based upon telephone interviews with local Qatari exchange houses on February 23, 2009. The day's average interbank exchange rate was QAR1 to NPR21.8929. Exchange Houses are designated as MTOs rather than banks.

Source: Authors' interviews with exchange houses.

typically dispatch checks to their agents. These checks are presented by the agents to their banks, and would need to be cleared as an out-station check if the agent and RSP are based in different locations. Alternatively, the remittance amount can be credited to the agent's account using manual credit transfers based on bilateral correspondent banking arrangements. However, these credit transfers are priced at NPR200, which is around 40 percent of the average service fee charged for remitting funds from Qatar to Nepal. RSPs typically aggregate their payments to agents to minimize this cost, which however may result in the agent having to be out-of-pocket for a longer period and charging the RSP a higher commission for that. It is likely that reducing this delay might enable the RSPs to lower the agent commission and hence potentially lower the price paid by the sender.

Notes

1. Qatar Central Bank and Qatar Statistics Authority.
2. Source: Nepal Rastra Bank.
3. Central Bureau of Statistics (CBS), Nepal.
4. As discussed earlier, the managed migration in this corridor means that most Nepali workers are documented, which gives them access to formal remittance service providers, as long as they present authorized identification documents (such as a passport or ID card issued by the Qatari government).
5. There are 14 conventional banks and 4 Islamic banks in Qatar.
6. It is important to note that banks do not compete directly with exchange houses for workers' remittances as banks mostly target remittances by high-skilled expatriates in Qatar.
7. QCB plans to draft regulations for mobile remittances based on its evaluation of the Vodafone Qatar pilot.
8. As opposed to the SMS-based platform which has a higher security risk and is costlier.

CHAPTER 3

The Regulatory Framework for Protecting the Integrity of Remittances

Regulations related to Anti-Money Laundering and Combating the Financing of Terrorism (AML/CFT) constitute a key component of the regulatory framework for remittances in any country and are key to protecting the integrity of these transfers. The Financial Action Task Force's (FATF) 40 Recommendations and 9 Special Recommendations set the international standards on AML/CFT. This chapter analyzes the regulatory framework for protecting the integrity of remittances in Qatar and Nepal and attempts to answer the following questions:

- *Who are the competent authorities that are regulating remittance service providers (particularly money transfer operators)?*
- *What are the licensing requirements for RSPs in both countries?*
- *What are the reporting requirements for remittance service providers?*
- *What are the customer identification and verification requirements?*
- *What are the challenges facing Qatar and Nepal in this area?*

In this corridor, remittance service providers, which include banks, remittance companies (in Nepal) and exchange houses (in Qatar) are regulated by competent authorities in both Qatar and Nepal. It is also important to note that as a result of managed migration in this corridor, the legal status of most migrant workers enables them to have an official identification card. This helps these workers fulfill the Know-Your-Customer (KYC) requirements of remittance service providers.

The Framework in Qatar

Legal and Regulatory Framework

The Central Bank Law of 2006 regulates remittance activities in Qatar. The Law defines foreign exchange activities as "exchanging and trading in different currencies, travelers' checks, ingots of precious metals, and the issuance and acceptance of remittances from licensed correspondents." Under the Law, banks and exchange houses are authorized to provide remittance services.[1] The QCB issues Directives to regulate these activities. Directives to banks cover, among other things, payment systems, public debt, banking operations, and AML/CFT. Directives to Exchange Houses prescribe, among other things, licensing requirements, operational guidance,[2] and AML/CFT.

In April 2010, a new AML/CFT Law (Law No 4. of 2010) was passed to strengthen the AML/CFT regime in Qatar. The new law replaced Law No. (28) of 2002 (Anti-Money Laundering Law) and Decree Law No. (21) of 2003 (Amendments to AML Law) which criminalized money laundering. Remittance service providers (only banks and exchange houses) are covered under the AML/CFT Law as part of the country's financial institutions. The Postal administration, although an issuer of money orders, is not covered by the Law.

Institutional Framework

The Qatar Central Bank is the regulator and supervisor of banks and exchange houses, which provide remittance services, and the Qatar Financial Information Unit is the national regulator and supervisor for AML/CFT. All remittance service providers are regulated by the QFIU for AML/CFT except for the postal service. Qatar is a member of Middle East and North Africa FATF (MENAFATF—a FATF-type regional organization) and a member of the Egmont Group, a group of financial intelligence units.

Licensing Requirements

Exchange houses are required to obtain a license to provide remittance services from the Qatar Central Bank. The license is renewed annually provided the exchange house satisfies all of QCB's requirements and pays two percent of its capital as well as an annual license fee of QAR5,000 for the principal office and QAR2,000 for each branch. Exchange Houses are not allowed to have agents. The main requirements for obtaining an exchange house license include, among others: a bank guarantee, proof of registration, and copies of the exchange house's by-laws and the contract of establishment.[3]

The Qatar Central Bank Law provides that financial services institutions, including exchange houses, must be joint stock companies and locally incorporated. The capital requirement for an exchange house license is set at QAR50 million. In 2006, the central bank removed a Qatari nationality requirement on ownership of financial institutions. However, as of 2009, no licenses had been granted under the amended Act.

Legal and Regulatory Requirements for AML/CFT

The new AML/CFT Law introduced a threshold for customer due diligence requirements for remittances and wire transfers. Any transactions under QAR4,000 ($1,100) do not require customer due diligence. This provision provides flexibility on customer due diligence (CDD) requirements, especially for migrant workers, most of whom send remittances of values lower than QAR4,000. It is important to highlight that the law requires suspicious transaction reports to be filed[4] regardless of the amount of transaction.

The new AML/CFT law also stipulates the requirements for customer identification. Article 30 of the new AML/CFT Law addresses specifically the CDD requirements for Exchange Houses. It requires financial institutions that provide money transfer services, whether domestically or cross-border, to get the following information for every transaction that exceeds QAR4,000: 1) Full name, 2) Account number, and 3) Address, or ID number, or the number identifying the customer, or date and place of birth.

QCB Directives (issued under the QCB Law) include specific measures for AML/CFT. There are a number of minor differences between the requirements of the new AML/CFT law and these QCB Directives, although they are not conflicting (FATF/MENAFATF, 2008). The QCB's Directives to exchange houses include requirements for, among others:

- Customer due diligence,
- Reporting of suspicious transactions to the FIU,
- Reporting cash transactions greater than QAR35,000, (under the new AML/CFT law, there are no cash transaction reporting requirements),

- Record keeping for 15 years (versus record keeping requirement for 5 years under the new AML/CFT law),
- Establishment of policies, procedures and internal controls to prevent money laundering and terrorism financing,
- Attention to companies and financial institutions from high risk countries, attention to complex and large transactions, and
- Appointment of a compliance officer responsible for AML/CFT matters.

The Framework in Nepal

Legal and Regulatory Framework

The Nepal Rastra Bank Act, 2058 (2002, amended in 2006), the Foreign Exchange Regulation Act of 1962, and Foreign Exchange Regulation Rules (1963) govern foreign exchange activities in Nepal. The NRB Act defines foreign exchange transactions as "the acts of purchase and sale of foreign exchange[5] or the acts of borrowing, giving credit, and of accepting or providing foreign exchange in any manner whatsoever." The Foreign Exchange Act of 1962 stipulates that remittance transfers should be treated as foreign exchange transactions. Under the Act, NRB has issued a circular which specifies the detailed licensing requirements for non-bank remittance service providers including: eligibility requirements, operating guidelines, reporting requirements, AML/CFT requirements and guarantee requirements. These laws, regulations, and directives issued by the Nepal Rastra Bank and its Financial Information Unit do not cover Nepal Post.

The Asset (Money) Laundering Prevention Act, 2064 (2008) and The Asset (Money) Laundering Prevention Rules, 2009 set the framework for Nepal's AML/CFT regime, which includes, among other things, criminalization of money laundering and financing of terrorism, customer identification requirements, the establishment of a national coordination committee and a Financial Information Unit (FIU) at NRB, and provisions for investigation and inquiry. With respect to remittances, the FIU has issued directives to banks and financial institutions (including MTOs) which prescribed requirements for, *inter alia*, customer identification, record keeping, currency transaction reporting (CTR), suspicious transaction reporting (STR), classification and mitigation of risks, and internal controls.

Institutional Framework

Nepal Rastra Bank is the regulator and supervisor of banks and remittance companies. The Financial Information Unit is the regulator for AML/CFT. At the policy level, the Coordination Committee provides recommendations to the Government of Nepal on AML/CFT. The Postal Service Department under the Ministry of Information and Communication is the regulator of Nepal Postal. Nepal is a member of Asia/Pacific Group on Money Laundering (APG—a FATF-type regional organization).

Licensing Requirements

Remittance companies are required to obtain a license to engage in international remittance transfers under the Foreign Exchange Regulation Act. According to the Act, a person, firm, company or corporation can apply for a license for foreign exchange transactions. The Money Changer Directive 2064 lists minimum licensing conditions including fit and proper criteria for the owners.

An NRB circular sets detailed licensing requirements for non-bank RSPs including: eligibility requirements, operating guidelines, reporting requirements, AML/CFT requirements and requires remittance service providers to present a bank guarantee ranging from NPR600,000 to NPR10 Million depending on the number of their agents. Annual licenses fees amount to NPR5,000. Remittance companies are also required to obtain an authorization for partnerships with companies in sending countries, supported by a signed agreement. International money transfer companies are not required to obtain a license, but their principal agents are.

Legal and Regulatory Requirements for AML/CFT

Customer identification requirements are established in the Asset (Money) Laundering Prevention Law. All reporting institutions[6] are required to identify a customer when establishing any kind of business relationship or transacting any amount above a certain threshold. The identification of customers is established by obtaining copies of identification cards, passports, and other necessary documents evidencing the permanent residence and profession or business of the client. All reporting institutions are required to keep a separate record of documents and transactions of each customer including date and nature of transactions, type of account, and account number. The Act, the Rules, and the Directives do not specify any duration of record keeping period although the international standards require record-keeping of at least five years.

The AML Directives to banks and to money transfer operators require remittance service providers to file currency transaction reports (CTRs) and suspicious transaction reports (STRs). With respect to currency transaction reporting requirements, the Asset (Money) Laundering Prevention Rules prescribes NRB's power to set thresholds for transactions. For foreign exchange transactions, banks are required to file a CTR on a transaction or multiple transactions of NPR500,000 or more by any person or entity in a day. Non-bank MTOs are required to file a CTR on a transaction or multiple transactions over NPR1 million per day. Currency transaction reports must be submitted to the Financial Information Unit within seven days, using a template provided as designated in the directives. Banks and remittance companies are required to immediately file suspicious transaction reports with the FIU. Both directives stipulate that there is no threshold or limit for reporting STRs.

Over the past two years, Nepal has significantly improved its AML/CFT regulatory framework for remittances. The Nepal Financial Information Unit has issued AML directives to banks/financial institution and MTOs in August and December 2009, respectively. This has ensured that AML/CFT requirements are being applied fairly to both banks and MTOs thereby keeping a level playing field. However, Nepal's AML/CFT regulatory framework on remittances is challenged by the still widely used unlicensed remittance services providers such as *Hundis*, especially for remittances from India. As the FATF Special Recommendation VI requires, such operators should also be registered/licensed or sanctioned in case they operate without official licensing.

Challenges in the Legal and Regulatory Framework of AML/CFT in Qatar and Nepal

Although the legal and regulatory framework for remittance services in both Nepal and Qatar seems conducive towards enhancing the integrity of these transfers, the following challenges remain.

The extensive use of *Hundi* for sending commissions from Nepal to Qatar raises integrity concerns. All these commissions are transferred from Nepal to Qatar through *Hundi,* which means they are unmonitored. These informal mechanisms could also be used for illegal purposes (such as money laundering). As described earlier, the use of *Hundi* for this purpose is induced by the illegality of such commissions in Qatar, the desire to avoid the TDS tax in Nepal, and capital controls imposed by NRB. Although the TDS tax rate was reduced, serious efforts have not have been made to reduce such transfers by reaching out to *Hundi* operators to encourage them to become regulated.

Anecdotal evidence suggests that identification cards issued by Qatari employers have been used for customer identification purposes by exchange houses although all migrant workers are supposed to have their own national passports and Qatari IDs. This practice raises concerns as to why official identification documents are not used. This may be due to the weak compliance capacity of exchange houses or to possible difficulties for migrant workers to present official identification documents (maybe because they lost their legal immigration status or their official documents are retained by their employers).

Nepali banks and money transfer operators appear to have weak compliance capacity and need more training of compliance officers. Over-reporting of STRs is taking place and could reflect weak compliance capacity and lack of proper understanding of STR filing. Reporting institutions, especially banks, tend to file suspicious transaction reports on transactions without proper internal analysis out of fear of being sanctioned for failing to report. However, compliance officers need to exercise a certain level of judgment: for example, a transaction with missing information does not need to be reported to the FIU if the bank can clear its suspicion by obtaining additional information from the customer.

Remittances through postal services (money orders) are not covered by the AML/CFT regulation in both Qatar and Nepal. Since money orders are not used in this corridor no risks have arisen so far. However, this loophole needs to be closed especially since both Q-Post and Nepal Post are Western Union's agents.

Finally, the licensing requirements in Nepal should ensure that only financially sound RSPs enter the market. In general recipients collect cash within maximum three days of the sender depositing funds with the RSP. During this period the RSP is holding the funds in its account. In case an RSP becomes insolvent, these pipeline funds are at-risk. To mitigate this risk, RSPs should be required to have adequate capital and guarantee funds to discharge their obligations. The current level of guarantees (mentioned earlier) might not be sufficient to cover the risk adequately, especially given the large size and wide geographical spread of some of these networks. It is also recommended that the NRB inspects non-bank RSPs regularly (which is not done now) in order to ensure that they are adhering to all the relevant regulations.

Notes

1. Exchange Houses are entities licensed to practice money exchange activities without receiving deposits.
2. For example, exchange houses are required to maintain reserves equal to the amount of remittance transactions over a certain period of time, for consumer protection purposes.
3. Instructions to Exchange Houses, 2006, Qatar Central Bank.
4. Under Article (18) of the AML/CFT Law, Reporting Entities and their personnel shall report promptly to the FIU any suspicious financial transactions or any attempts to perform such

transactions, regardless of the amount of the transaction, in the following circumstances: A) when they suspect or have reasonable grounds to suspect that these transactions include funds that are proceeds of a criminal activity, or B) are linked or related to, or to be used for terrorist acts or by terrorist organizations or those who finance terror.

5. In the Act, "Foreign Exchange" is defined as foreign currencies, all types of deposits, credits, stocks, foreign securities payable in foreign currencies and the checks, drafts, traveler's checks, electronic fund transfer, credit cards, letters of credit, bills of exchange, promissory notes in international circulation payable in foreign currencies; and the word also includes whatsoever, types of other monetary instrument as the Bank may prescribe, as per the requirement, by publication and transmission of public notices.

6. Reporting institutions are banks, financial institutions, non-financial institutions, and government entities having obligation to report information and particulars to the FIU as per the provisions of the Act.

CHAPTER 4

Conclusions and Policy Recommendations

This chapter highlights the main findings of the report's analysis and provides policy recommendations to address the identified challenges. In certain cases, the experiences of other countries are shared as potentially useful best practice examples. Both Qatar and Nepal have already implemented significant initiatives aimed at enhancing the efficiency, transparency and effectiveness of the migration and remittance transfer process between the two countries. For example, Qatar has developed high-tech procedures to process visa applications. Nepal has been pro-active in adjusting regulations affecting remittance transfers and improving their integrity. Nepal has also been promoting formal migration agreements with the main host countries for Nepali migrants, such as Qatar and Malaysia. These activities have already provided a basis for both countries to engage in a dialogue to maximize the benefits of migration on remittances for both sides.

The policy recommendations present areas where Qatari and Nepali authorities could, independently or jointly, take the necessary actions. These recommendations focus on:

- Streamlining inefficiencies in the migration process from Nepal to Qatar,
- Improving the scale and impact of remittance transfers from Qatar to Nepal, and
- Enhancing the integrity of migration and remittances in the corridor.

Migration-related Findings & Policy Recommendations

High Migration Costs, which Force Migrants to Borrow to Finance their Migration

As highlighted in chapter one, it seems that contrary to the rules and regulations governing the migration process from Nepal to Qatar, Nepali workers end up paying high migration fees to manpower agencies. The problem is caused by discrepancies between regulations, lack of enforcement of these regulations and the bilateral agreement, as well as an unclear mix of legitimate and illegitimate fees. Lack of awareness among migrant workers exacerbates the problem. As per the Qatar Labor Law and the Qatar-Nepal Bilateral Agreement, payments by migrants or Nepali middlemen for travel expenses and commissions to Qatari recruitment service companies are illegal. The Qatari employer had to pay these costs. However, Nepali regulations allow Nepali manpower agencies to collect such fees up to a ceiling of NPR70,000. In reality, the total cost of migration for Nepali workers averages around US$1,216. It takes on average 4–6 months' salary for a Nepali working in the service industry in Qatar to recover this cost. *In order to pay for migration, Nepali workers borrow money from their family members and in 43 percent of the cases from local moneylenders* (who charge high interest rates). As a result, remittances sent by migrant workers during the first year are typically used to repay migration loans, limiting the amount of funds available for their families.

33

Transfers of Commissions through Informal Funds Transfer (IFT) Systems

The current migration process has prompted informal funds flows from Nepal to Qatar, in order to transfer the commissions of middlemen and recruitment service companies. Nepali manpower agencies use Hundi to transfer these commissions in order to avoid paying the required Tax Deductions at the Payment Source (TDS), and to avoid seeking NRB approval for what is a capital outflow from Nepal. In their turn, Qatari recruitment service companies prefer to receive these commissions through informal methods since these commissions are illegal in Qatar. In addition, there appears to be many unlicensed or unauthorized middlemen providing migrant services in both countries, who prefer to use IFT systems. The size of these commission flows is estimated to range from US$17 million to US$34 million per annum, amounting to around 5 percent of recorded worker remittance flows from Qatar to Nepal.

Recommendations for Streamlining Inefficiencies in the Migration Process

While meeting a critical need to place workers with firms, the existence of middlemen and manpower agencies in the Qatar-Nepal Remittance Corridor has fostered an environment of illegal activities and high fees. Ultimately, the migrant worker bears the brunt of this as higher migration costs. To the extent that the Nepali and Qatari governments are able to exercise better oversight and improve coordination, this illegal activity can diminish to the benefit of migrant workers.

1. *Qatari and Nepali authorities should clarify all the steps, procedures, fees and responsibilities involved in the migration process from Nepal to Qatar.* This will minimize abuse and help ensure that all entities involved in the process are held accountable. A mutually agreed and jointly issued set of guidelines on migration could include information about the migration process, the necessary steps, the parties involved, the required fees, as well as the parties that are legally obliged to pay these fees. This will help ensure that migrant workers, recruitment agencies, recruitment service companies and Qatari companies are clear about the procedures/fees involved and thus do not pay any illegitimate fees. Increased transparency in the migration process will also help reduce the use of illegal middlemen. In addition, the Qatari government should create awareness about and enforce the regulations that stipulate that commissions to Qatari recruitment service companies by Nepali migrants or recruitment companies are prohibited. Once commissions to Qatari recruitment service companies are stopped, the use of Hundi to transfer these commissions will cease.

2. *Qatari and Nepali authorities should enforce the bilateral agreement.* This will significantly reduce the high migration costs by ensuring that migrant workers are not charged airfare expenses. The Nepali authorities could then consider revising the ceiling of NPR70,000 for migration to Qatar (since it includes unnecessary airfare and an illegal commission). The enforcement of the bilateral agreement will also allow the Embassy of Nepal to be the only authority which would attest all contracts, which will also result in ensuring minimum wages for Nepali workers.

3. *Nepali authorities should endeavor to empower migrant workers by equipping them with information on the migration process, fees, and responsibilities, and should provide them with financial education.* This will help them avoid paying unnecessary expenses during the migration process, and getting indebted to finance this migration. In particular, given the large number of Nepali migrants heading to Qatar, as

Box 4.1. Financing of Migration: An Example from Indonesia

A savings bank in Indonesia—Bank Rakyat Indonesia (BRI)—developed a loan product for financing the migration of Indonesian workers who are migrating to work for a contracted employer in Malaysia. The bank offers credit to the migrants at the time of departure, which is secured with a solidarity group. The employer directly makes repayment to a recruitment agency which collectively pays dues to the savings bank. The recruitment agency provides a guarantee of repayment. The recruitment agency purchases an insurance policy for the payments in case workers run away from the employment. It is important to note that the Bank of Indonesia (the central bank) has issued a guideline on this scheme. According to the savings bank, the repayment rate for this scheme was very high (almost 100 percent). At the time of the interview, the interest rate of the product was 1.25 percent per month.

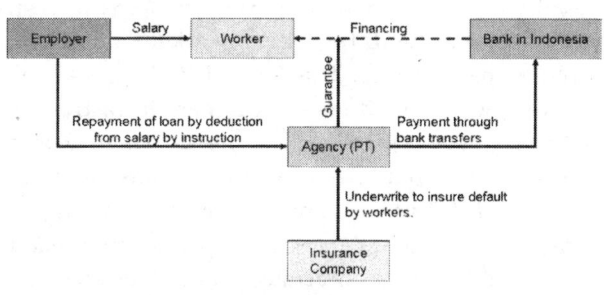

Source: BRCA fieldwork for the Malaysia-Indonesia Remittance Corridor report.

well as the importance of remittance flows from Qatar to Nepal, these financial education and literacy programs should be tailored to the Qatari context, for those migrants heading to Qatar. Information could include options about financial services in Qatar, how to access them, and tips on sending money home from Qatar. In addition, some effort should be excreted to help migrants educate their own families in Nepal on options for accessing remittances as well as potential financial services linked to them.

4. *Nepali authorities should encourage the development of commercially-viable and sustainable non-collateral-based migration financing schemes.* The example of a scheme from Indonesia (see box 4.1) could be replicated in Nepal, whereby banks lend migrants based on a collective repayment guarantee by their manpower agency which is repaid directly by the foreign employer through monthly deductions from the migrants' salaries. Partnerships with MFI could also be piloted to expand the reach of such loans.

Remittance Transfers-related Findings & Policy Recommendations

Most remittances from Qatar to Nepal are transmitted through formal financial institutions such as exchange houses (MTOs) and banks. The gradual reduction in remittance transfer costs in this corridor has been accelerated by intense competition and increased volumes.

Limited RSP Coverage Outside Doha and Limited Enthusiasm of Qatari Banks

Although RSPs in Qatar can now establish more than two branches (in addition to their main office), the new regulations have only recently taken effect and there remains limited RSP coverage outside Doha. Most Nepali migrant workers still feel compelled to travel to Doha to send remittances. Some migrant workers live near oil mining locations (where they do not have access to any formal remittance service providers) therefore, their employers usually arrange a bus service for them to travel to Doha during their free time on Fridays. In general, Qatari banks are not interested in entering the remittance market because they believe that remittance services are less profitable than other services, and because they are focused on corporate lending. Since the services offered by exchange houses are cash-based services, this means that many Nepali migrant workers do not have the opportunity to access savings accounts, which could provide them with safety and enable them access to other financial services.

Limited Development of the Domestic Payment System Infrastructure in Nepal

Nepal is a cash-based economy and the payment systems infrastructure is under-developed. There is no electronic funds transfer network for interbank payments. Checks are cleared manually and paper-based. This has led RSPs to maintain large agent networks to pay cash to recipients. The domestic payment infrastructure is used by RSPs to transfer funds to their agents, typically using checks. These checks are presented by the agents to their banks, and would need to be cleared as an out-station check if the agent and RSP are based in different locations (requiring up to 7 days). Alternatively, the remittance amount can be credited to the agent's account using manual credit transfers based on bilateral correspondent banking arrangements. However, these credit transfers cost around 40 percent of the average service fee charged for remitting funds from Qatar to Nepal. RSPs typically aggregate their payments to agents to minimize this cost, which however may result in the agent having to be out-of-pocket for a longer period and thus charging the RSP higher commissions.

Recommendations for Improving the Scale and Impact of Remittance Transfers

1. *Nepali authorities should expand and upgrade the domestic payment systems and remittance distribution network in Nepal.* They could do so by encouraging banks to increase banking penetration (especially in rural areas) using new technology such as mobile payment schemes, prepaid cards and branchless banking solutions. They should also promote the development of an Automated Transfer System for credit transfers which would enable RSPs to move funds to their agents faster and process credit-to-account remittances efficiently. Finally, all stakeholders in Nepal should build the capacity of the postal system and automate it, to leverage its extensive network for providing payment and remittance services.

2. *Qatar Central Bank should encourage exchange houses to open new branches closer to migrant workers locations.* This would reduce the need for migrant workers to travel to Doha to send remittances, thereby minimizing the risks of carrying cash. It would also reduce the need for IFT operators or other community-based arrangements to send remittances.

3. *Qatari authorities should encourage Qatari firms to open bank accounts for their workers and deposit their salaries in those accounts.* The use of bank accounts to deposit salaries could reduce Qatari firms' costs of handling cash and would increase workers' security. This would also provide an incentive to banks to provide more financial services to migrant workers', thereby allowing them to enter this hitherto untapped market.

4. *Nepali and Qatari authorities should encourage Nepali banks and financial institutions that have an extensive presence in Nepal (especially in rural areas) to operate in Qatar.*

This will allow them to service both ends of the market by providing services to the migrants in Qatar and Nepal, before and after migration, as well as to the migrants' families in Nepal after migration. This could help ensure that remittances are leveraged to improve access to financial services.

5. *Qatari and Nepali authorities should consider supporting the development of remittance services through mobile phones.* This can be done by developing an appropriate regulatory framework to support such a development in consultation with the private sector, and based on the best practices from other countries' experiences in this field (such as the Philippines). It is important to draft appropriate regulations that effectively mitigate integrity risks without constraining the ability of mobile money providers to efficiently and rapidly expand access to financial services among low income populations.

Regulatory Framework-related Findings & Policy Recommendations

Both Qatar and Nepal's AML/CFT framework on remittances seems to be fairly comprehensive and ensures the integrity of the transfer process. However, the continued use of *Hundi* for sending migration commission raises integrity concern. In addition, remittance transfers through postal services (money orders) are not covered by the AML/CFT regulation in both Qatar and Nepal.

Nepali banks and money transfer operators appear to have weak compliance capacity and need more training of compliance officers. Over-reporting of STRs is taking place and could reflect weak compliance capacity and lack of proper understanding of STR filing.

Finally, the licensing requirements in Nepal should ensure that only financially sound RSPs enter the market. The current level of bank guarantee might not be adequate to cover the liquidity risk of large RSPs, especially given the predominance of cash pay-outs.

Policy Recommendations

1. *Both Qatari and Nepali authorities should engage in efforts to reach out to IFT operators in order to raise their awareness about the illegality of their activities and encourage them to get licensed.* Although implementing the above-mentioned policy recommendation on the migration process would eliminate much of the reasons to use these operators, the authorities should still engage with them to get them licensed.

2. *Both Qatari and Nepali authorities should provide effective training on AML/CFT requirements to banks, money transfer operators and other reporting institutions.* Since Qatar's new AML/CFT Law came into effect in April 2010, the authorities should raise awareness about the new regime and ensure its implementation. Likewise, Nepal's FIU recently issued many guidelines under its AML/CFT law. Proper training and awareness raising among the industry is a key success factor for an effective AML/CFT regime.

3. *The NRB should consider raising the current level of bank guarantee required by non-bank RSPs and should intensify its supervision of these institutions,* in order to mitigate potential liquidity risks, especially given the large agent networks in Nepal, and the predominance of cash-pay-outs throughout these, sometimes remote, networks.

Payment System Platforms in the Remittance Corridor

In order to offer cheap, fast, secure and reliable remittance services, it is of great importance to develop the infrastructure for international remittance transfers. Remittance transactions use the payment system infrastructure of both Qatar and Nepal. This transfer usually happens in two stages (see below for more details):

- Movement of funds from Nepali RSP's Qatari partner to the RSPs "Nostro" account in a foreign country usually USA. In the case of international MTOs, it is movement of funds from the MTO to its Nepali principal agents' "Nostro" account in a foreign country. This generally uses the SWIFT network.
- Movement of funds from the "Nostro" account to a bank account in Nepal. This involves foreign exchange conversion into Nepali Rupees, and uses the standard correspondent banking arrangements.

Cross-Border Payments and Settlement Examples

There are several methods of remittance transfers and settlements. Differences are observed in transmission of information and funds for a remittance transaction from a collecting to a disbursing RSPs. The charts below illustrate simplified flows of information and funds. Transmissions of funds between domestic banks usually go through domestic payment systems. Diagram A-1 illustrates typical domestic funds transfer from one bank to another through domestic payment systems. Since both the QAR and NPR are not internationally traded currencies, settlement arrangements are made in US dollars in a bank in the US. Below are descriptions of the following formal remittance channels:

- Exchange House—MTO Transfer
- Bank—Bank Transfer with Partnership
- Regular Bank—Bank Transfer

Exchange House—MTO Transfer

Diagram A-2 explains a remittance transfer from an exchange house in Qatar to an MTO in Nepal. The exchange house captures funds and information from a sender and transmits funds through a correspondent bank while sending the information of the transaction directly to the MTO in Nepal. The MTO disburses payments to a recipient as soon as it receives the instruction. Settlement takes place usually in the next few days.

Diagram A-1

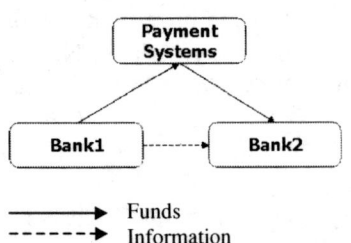

Funds
------ Information

38

Diagram A-2

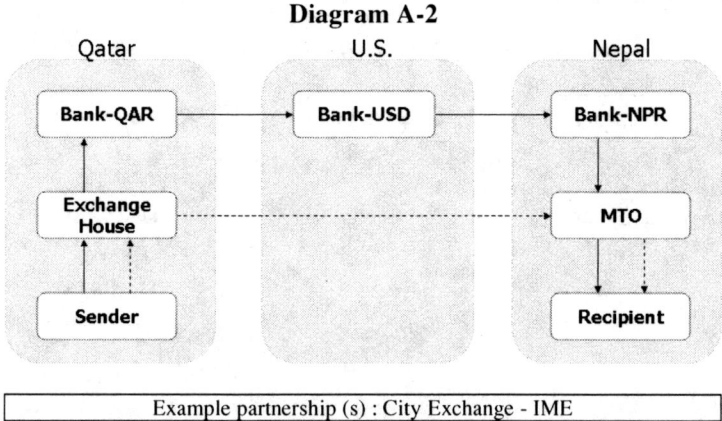

Example partnership (s) : City Exchange - IME

Bank-Bank Transfer with Partnership

In Diagram A-3, capturing and disbursing RSPs are banks. A bank in Qatar receives funds and information from a sender. The bank in Qatar transfers funds to a receiving bank in Nepal through a bank in the US, and transmits information directly to the receiving bank. The bank in Nepal disburses funds to a recipient as soon as the information arrives.

Regular Bank to Bank Transfer

Diagram A-4 displays a normal bank to bank transfer mechanism. This type of transfer is rather rare for workers' remittances in the Qatar-Nepal corridor.

Diagram A-3

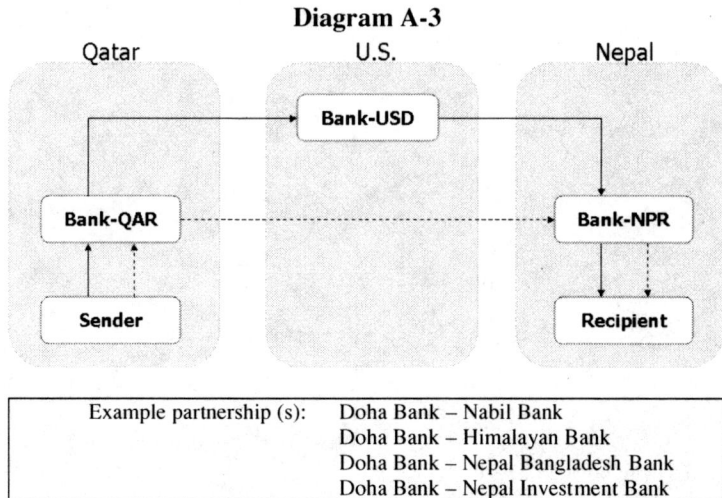

Example partnership (s):   Doha Bank – Nabil Bank
                             Doha Bank – Himalayan Bank
                             Doha Bank – Nepal Bangladesh Bank
                             Doha Bank – Nepal Investment Bank

Diagram A-4

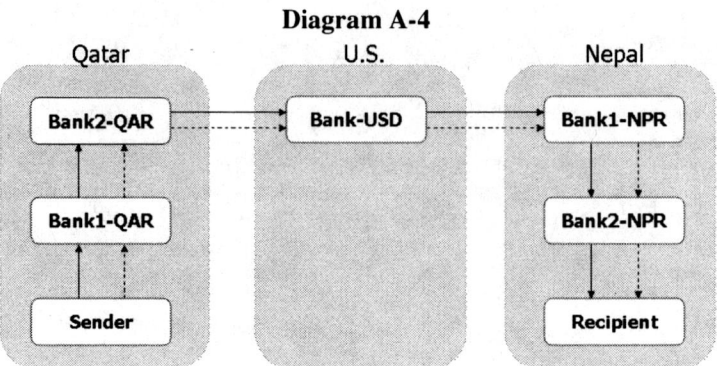

Bibliography

Baldwin-Edwards, M. 2005. "Migration in the Middle East and Mediterranean." Paper prepared for the Policy Analysis and Research Programme of the Global Commission on International Migration (GCIM), September. <http://www.gcim.org/attachements/RS5.pdf>.

Beck, Thorsten, and María Soledad Martínez Pería. 2009. "What Explains the Cost of Remittances? An Examination across 119 Country Corridors." Policy Research Working Paper 5072. Washington, D.C.: The World Bank.

Economist Intelligence Unit. 2010. *Country Report: Qatar.* London.

FATF/MENAFATF. 2008. Mutual Evaluation Report: Anti-Money Laundering and Combating the Financing of Terrorism. Qatar.

Government of Qatar. 2006. Law No. "33" of the Year 2006. Qatar Central Bank.

Government of Nepal. 1962. Foreign Exchange (Regulation) Act, 1962.

———. 2002. Nepal Rastra Bank Act, 2058 (2002).

———. 2007a. Money Changer Directive, 2064.

———. 2007b. Foreign Employment Act, 2064.

———. 2007c. Foreign Employment Regulation, 2064.

———. 2008. Asset (Money) Laundering Prevention Act, 2008.

———. 2009. Asset (Money) Laundering Prevention Rules, 2009.

IMF. 2009. Executive Board Concludes 2008 Article IV Consultation with the United Arab Emirates, Public Information Notice (PIN) No. 09/47.

International Organization for Migration. 2003. *Labour Migration in Asia: Trends, challenges and policy responses in countries of origin.* <http://www.iom.int/DOCUMENTS/PUBLICATION/EN/LabourMigAsia.pdf>.

———. 2005. "International Migration Trends," Chapter 23 in *World Migration 2005: Costs and Benefits of International Migration.*

Kansakar, Vidya Bir Singh. 2001. "Nepal-India Open Border: Prospects, Problems and Challenges." Nepal Democracy. <http://www.nepaldemocracy.org/>.

———. 2003. "International Migration and Citizenship in Nepal," Chapter 14 in *Population Monograph of Nepal.* Kathmandu, Nepal: Central Bureau of Statistics and UNFPA.

———. 2005. *Nepal India Migration and Remittances.*

Kapiszewski, Andrezej. 2006. "Arab versus Asian Migrant Workers in the GCC Countries." United Nations Department of Economic and Social Affairs, Population Division. New York.

Nepal Post. 2004. *Annual Report 2002 & 2003.* Kathmandu, Nepal.

Nepal Rastra Bank. 2005. *Banking and Financial Statistics* 45(July). <http://www.nrb.org.np/bfr/statistics/Banking_and_Financial_Statistics—No_45_July_2005.pdf>.

OECD. 2005. *Migration, Remittances and Development: The Development Dimension.* Paris.

Paudel, Dandapani. 2005. "Financial Sector Development," in *Nepal Rastra Bank in Fifty Years*. Nepal Rastra Bank.

Qatar Central Bank. 1995. *Decree Law No. (36) of the Year 1995 Regarding Regulating of Money Exchange Business*.

———. 2005a. "Qatar Central Bank Payment System Features (QPS)." Website accessed November 12. <http://www.qcb.gov.qa/pages/English_Site/QPS.html>.

———. 2005b. *Twenty Eighth Annual Report 2004*. Doha, Qatar.

———. 2008. *Thirty First Annual Report 2007*. Doha, Qatar

———. 2009. The *Thirty Second Annual Report*.

Qatar Statistics Authority. 2010. Labour Force Sample Survey 2009. Doha, Qatar.

Ratha, Dilip. Forthcoming. "Migrant Remittances in Nepal: Best Practices and Policy Options." Washington, D.C.: The World Bank.

Ratha, Dilip, Sanket Mohapatra, and Ani Silwal. 2009. "Migration and Remittance Trends 2009: A better-than-expected outcome so far, but significant risks ahead." Migration and Development Brief 11. The World Bank, Washington, D.C.

United Nations. 2005. *Trends in Total Migrant Stock: the 2005 Revision*. Department of Economic and Social Affairs, Population Division. New York. http://esa.un.org/migration.

———. 2009. *Trends in International Migrant Stock: The 2008 Revision*. Department of Economic and Social Affairs, Population Division (United Nations database, POP/DB/MIG/Stock/Rev.2008). New York.

World Bank. 2006. "The Impact of Migration and Remittances. Resilience amidst Conflict: An Assessment of Poverty in Nepal, 1995–96 and 2003–04." Washington, D.C.

———. 2008. *Migration and Remittances Factbook 2008*. Washington, D.C.